Many Christians believe in eternity yet have no real understanding about the afterlife. Few of us will experience it until our earthly bodies fail us once and for all. But Freddy Vest has not only experienced a taste of heaven, he has also come back to tell us about it. His fascinating and true story, *The Day I Died*, will convince skeptic and believer alike that heaven is a real and wonderful place and that God is a real person—One who loves us, has compassion for us, and hears and answers our prayers.

—PAT ROBERTSON
Founder/chairman, The Christian Broadcasting Network

THE
DAY
I
DIED

FREDDY VEST

CHARISMA
HOUSE

Most CHARISMA HOUSE BOOK GROUP products are available at special quantity discounts for bulk purchase for sales promotions, premiums, fund-raising, and educational needs. For details, write Charisma House Book Group, 600 Rinehart Road, Lake Mary, Florida 32746, or telephone (407) 333-0600.

THE DAY I DIED by Freddy Vest
Published by Charisma House
Charisma Media/Charisma House Book Group
600 Rinehart Road
Lake Mary, Florida 32746
www.charismahouse.com

Cover design by Lisa Rae Cox
Design Director: Bill Johnson

To learn more about Freddy Vest, visit www.charismahouse.com.

Library of Congress Control Number: 2014936503
International Standard Book Number: 978-1-62136-544-0
E-book ISBN: 978-1-62136-545-7

First edition

14 15 16 17 18 — 9 8 7 6 5 4 3 2 1
Printed in the United States of America

I would like to dedicate this book to all who are hurting and feeling the pain of losing someone very close to them ... and to those diagnosed with terminal illnesses, who understand that their time on Earth is short, but have hope that something far better awaits them.

THE OLD COWBOY'S ROPE

There was an old cowboy riding on his way,
seeing an old church house, his respects there to pay.

His hat was tattered, his jeans had a hole,
his boots were worn, but his spurs still had their jingle.

He took the back pew as a young cowboy took notice
of the old man holding his rope through the service,
gentle and respectful, as though it were his best friend.

When the younger man could stand it no more
he asked the old cowboy about his rope.

The older man answered, his voice atremble,
"Son, this old rope has been with me most of my life.

It was there when I was cold and wet.
It helped feed me when I was hungry.

And when I was busted up at the bottom of the ravine,
this rope is what I used to pull myself up.

You see, son, when I look at this rope
I see the Father, Son, and Holy Ghost.

The rope is made from three strong strands:
In one I see God All-Knowing, His name is Jehovah.
In another, God All-Giving, His name is Jesus.
In the third I see God All-Personal, His name is Holy
    Spirit.

Each strand alone is strong, but intertwined
    unbreakable.

Together it is called God the Holy Trinity
This old rope is more than my Best Friend; it is the only
    Bible I have."

When the service was over, they stood up to leave.
The young cowboy, holding his Bible, handed it to the
    older man,
who stood for a moment with tears in his eyes.

He asked the young cowboy, "Would you do me a favor?
My days are short but this rope is not done.
Will you take it and cherish it as a new friend?

May it remind you of the One watching over you,
just as it has done for me for so long."

As the years passed, the young cowboy understood
what the old cowboy had passed along.

The younger could not see that rope without seeing God
and giving thanks for all He had done.

"The rope was with me when I was cold and wet.
It fed me when I was hungry,
and comforted me at the bottom of the ravine."

Those words ring true with every glance at that old
    rope—
For, you see, that young cowboy was me.

—FREDDY VEST

CONTENTS

ACKNOWLEDGMENTS

I WOULD LIKE TO thank all who had a part in my return from heaven: Eddy Smith, Kathy Glover, Don Lavendor, Dennis McKinley, Nick Burnham, the Graham first responders, the CareFlite pilot and EMTs, the staff at Harris Methodist Hospital, and all the cowboys and others who prayed for me and for my recovery.

The list goes on and on; there are many more folks than I can mention individually.

I would like to thank my family for never giving up on me and for being there when I needed them most.

Sincere thanks also to the Christian Broadcasting Network (CBN) and Pat Robertson for their support in producing and airing the reenactment of my story, and to Amy Reid for her careful attention in producing the video.

Thank you to Maureen Eha and Charisma Media for this amazing opportunity to tell my story, as my mother would say, "warts and all." This was God's plan all the way, and Maureen and Charisma are a beautiful part of it.

Also, I would like to thank Donna Scuderi for helping to put my words in print. Without her this book would not have been possible.

I must also acknowledge my mother and dad for their love and direction in my life.

Most of all, I must thank my God for choosing me to tell this story and give Him the glory for all things.

May this story bear witness that heaven is real, and God is too.

~~ Chapter 1 ~~

COWBOYS and ANGELS

"Go to the village ahead of you, and just as you enter it, you will find a colt tied there, which no one has ever ridden. Untie it and bring it here."... When they brought the colt to Jesus and threw their cloaks over it, he sat on it. [You see, Jesus was the first real cowboy.]
MARK 11:2, 7

YOU DON'T ALWAYS see your last breath coming. I knew that was true before July 26, 2008, but not as I know it now. Not even close.[1]

That morning, there was no hint that my last breath was near. It was another great day to rodeo. Every day is a great day to rodeo. A scorcher was shaping up in Texas, and I was planning on roping some calves. The weatherman predicted temperatures north of 100 degrees, and he was right. The high of the day would hit 108. Oxygen seemed scarce, and sweat was easy to come by. But neither heat nor perspiration would keep me from roping. Almost nothing could keep me from that.

One thing was different that morning: I woke up alone. My wife, Debbie, and our son Colton were in Mississippi visiting family. They left the day before and already I missed them. My daughter, Leigh, and I had business to look after, so we stayed home. I wasn't scheduled to rope till afternoon, so I fed the horses and did some chores in the barn.

By 10:00 a.m., I'd loaded the trailer, and my horse, Rapture, and I were ready to roll. Leigh, the sweet "baby" of our family, saw me to the door. We hugged extra long and hard that morning. Neither of us could say why, but we shared the sense that there was a reason—an unknown but undeniable reason why this hug was so special. Without words, we savored it and let go after a while. I told Leigh how much I loved her. Then I turned to walk away.

Leigh called after me and said, "I love you, Daddy." I thought I saw her eyes well up just a little. A couple of tears tried coming loose from my eyes too. It was a moment to cherish, but it was also time to go. So I turned and headed for the rodeo.

ALMOST AN ORDINARY DAY

The two-hour drive to Graham, Texas, was uneventful. Temperatures continued climbing, but the arena in Graham was covered. There would be some relief from the heat but not much.

Pretty soon my gear was unloaded, and I was saddled up, ready to rope. There was a session of ropers ahead of me, so I grabbed a rodeo taco, a Coke, and a Snickers bar, and visited with my buddy Nick Burnham in the stands. Nick is a cowboy and veterinarian. The two of us have roped together over the years. Nick and his wife live about ten miles from Debbie and me. They are super people and very good friends.

Nick and I talked awhile as I downed my lunch and waited my turn at roping. Pretty soon it was game on, and my first run went well. Out of forty-five entries, I won the round with the fastest time. My second calf wasn't as cooperative, at least not enough for a win. Still, my average time was high enough for my third run to matter.

A few seconds is what it takes to win in calf roping. A lot has to happen in that sliver of time, so you have to know what your calf is going to do. He starts out with a lead of ten feet or so. You have to keep that distance apart or lose the run. It's trickier than it sounds, for you and your horse. Some calves break hard out of the chute, charging forward at a steady clip. If your calf runs straight, it's even better and easier to judge your speed. But if he ducks and dives, it makes a good run more challenging. Break that ten-foot barrier, and your run is a washout.

When it was time for my third run, I knew which calf I was up against. My good friend Dave Martin was sitting on the fence near the chute. Dave knows how critical those few seconds are and how important it is to get your calf out quick. He called to me and asked, "Do you need a push?"

That calf had given me trouble once before, so I said, "Yes, thanks. Go ahead and give a push."

Dave got in behind the calf and pushed him toward the gate. He came out quick enough, but once again, he gave me a tough time. He was hard to flank,[2] fighting hard to stay upright. Once I got him down, he wouldn't take a tie.[3] Fifteen seconds later, I had him wrapped up; but the win was long gone.

After a loss, I run down my mental checklist. My horse is my partner, so the checklist covers both of us. A good scoring horse is alert and able to resist instinct and keep the rope tight. I wondered whether my horse had worked enough rope on this run, and whether I'd kept my part of the bargain. It was a mystery to me why this calf was so hard to handle.

There would be more time for questions later. For now I needed to make way for the next roper and get ready for my fourth calf. Because of the high temperatures and a difficult third run, I felt tired—not unusually tired, but the way anyone would feel after wrestling a 250-pound animal that wants to break free. Overall, I felt as good as ever. I was a working cowboy who had gone to the mat doing what he loves. So I put the run behind me, mounted my horse, and looked forward to calf number four.

As I waited, I shot the breeze with another friend. Then suddenly, without warning, it was lights out. I, Freddy Vest, was dead before my body hit the ground.

COWBOY DOWN

I don't know exactly what happened next, so I asked my friend Donna to help me share this part of my story.

Those nearest Freddy knew soon enough that he hadn't fainted. He was gone. His cowboy preacher friend, Dennis McKinley, was sitting on a fence nearby when Freddy checked out. Out of the corner of his eye Dennis saw sudden movement and heard a loud crack. Freddy had fallen from his horse, his body smacking hard against the ground.

Dennis leaped off the fence and ran to Freddy. He cradled his friend's head and prayed as a call went out for someone to administer CPR. Eddy Smith, a Dallas firefighter, responded first. Immediately he took control of the situation and began chest compressions. A nurse named Kathy Glover worked alongside Eddy, breathing for Freddy until another firefighter, Don Lavendor, asked to take over.

Eddy and Don were longtime friends of Freddy's who knew exactly what to do. Meanwhile, Dennis asked everyone to pray. Prayers were heard coming from every direction. Dozens of people remained on their knees. Eddy prayed too, never missing a compression or losing focus. The symphony of prayers kept him motivated. He figured that as long as people kept praying, he would keep trying to restart Freddy's heart.

Dave Martin, the cowboy who pushed Freddy's third calf out of the chute, didn't know anything to do besides pray. But pray he could, and pray he did.

A DEAD MAN

Eddy and Don knew a dead man when they saw one. Both were seasoned first responders. Don's firehouse happened to be near a nursing home. Calls to 911 were common. So was death. Now his friend was dead, and all Don could do was force breath into his lungs on the outside chance that the resuscitation would "take."

There was no sign it was working, but it was all Eddy and Don had to give. They knew it was Freddy's only chance. Eddy pounded the chest of his ashen friend relentlessly. A shaken bystander scolded him for working it so hard. "You're going to hurt him!" she shouted.

"You can't hurt a dead man," said Eddy.

He knew that breaking the breastbone was necessary for effective CPR. He also knew the fracture was the least of Freddy's problems.

FORTY-FIVE-MINUTE CLOCK

Forty-five minutes would elapse before an ambulance arrived. Eddy and Don worked on Freddy every minute of that time, pausing only for Nick Burnham to check Freddy's pulse. Each time Nick's answer was the same: "There's nothing."

The men never gave up. They tried longer than most anyone would have deemed reasonable. Had they surrendered, no one would have thought any less of them. But quitting was not in their DNA. They were determined to give Freddy every possible chance to make it.

As Freddy says, "Cowboys never quit."

And they didn't quit, not even when the clock ran out, and Freddy was too far gone.

Eddy had another issue on his plate that day. A month earlier he had judged one of Freddy's roping runs, one that ended badly. Freddy was unhappy with the call and questioned it. After years of rodeo and friendship under their belts, the men hashed out their differences, but they kept things in perspective. Right and wrong were not at issue. This was a matter of professional opinions—strong opinions.

It remained a sticky subject. Earlier on the day Freddy died, Eddy made a comment that stirred the pot. It was enough to draw Freddy's fire. He looked at Eddy and said, "You can't pick your judges, but you can pick your friends."

Freddy made his point, and Eddy knew exactly where he was coming from.

Even if Eddy felt put out, it did not stop him from doing the right thing. For the full forty-five minutes before the ambulance arrived, he kept working on Freddy. He never asked anyone to take over the chest compressions; he never even let anyone try. As long as Eddy had access to his friend's body, he would give all he had to revive him.

When the ambulance reached the arena, paramedics found Eddy very much in control. His "shift" was officially over, but he would not call it a day. This mildly irritated the EMTs. Still, Eddy did not relent. Instead, he insisted that they continue chest compressions. He also requested that they use a backboard to provide added support and make the compressions more effective.

Everyone knew Freddy had been dead a long time, but Eddy maintained his stand: he wanted his replacements to fight for Freddy as fiercely as he and Don had.

Eddy watched the EMTs' every move. When they connected Freddy to the heart monitor, he saw on the screen what he already knew: Freddy had flatlined.

Dennis asked Eddy, "What does that mean?"

"It means he's dead," Eddy replied.

The paramedics applied the paddles to shock Freddy's heart into rhythm. Nothing happened, so they tried again. Again, the treatment failed.

ONLY GOD

Freddy's friends watched and prayed. They had done all they could for as long as they could. Whether life or death, the outcome was beyond their control. The one thing left to do was to leave Freddy in God's hands. Only He could help their friend now.

Paramedics resumed chest compressions as the ambulance drove away. Once it exited the arena and entered the parking lot outside, it rolled to a stop. The emergency lights quit flashing, and the vehicle began moving again but slowly.

To Freddy's friends, it was a bad sign.

Nick Burnham followed the ambulance anyway. When he arrived at the ER, a paramedic said the words Nick hoped never to hear: "Sorry, Nick. I'm pretty sure your friend didn't make it."

Back in Mississippi, Debbie and Colton were at a

cousin's house enjoying burgers and fellowship when a friend called with bad news. She said the details were sketchy, but she knew this much: Freddy had fallen from his horse, and it didn't look good.

~Chapter 2~

REARED in the FAITH

Start children off on the way they should go, and
even when they are old they will not turn from it.
PROVERBS 22:6

M OST PEOPLE DON'T know the day they're going to die. I certainly never expected to die so soon; but I was prepared, and had been for years. I certainly don't have it all figured out, but I have learned some things about life and death.

MAMA, DADDY, AND EVERYDAY MIRACLES

There was no way to grow up in our family and not believe in miracles. From the time I was old enough to comprehend, I saw all kinds of miracles. Many of them would have been overlooked by other families. But we Vests knew how miraculous they were. Every miracle mattered, and every one left a mark on my siblings and me.

Being the seventeenth of eighteen children born to sharecroppers was probably the first miracle of my life.

Not that it ever seemed unusual to me. Coming from a large family was all I knew. But after raising a family of my own, the idea of sharecroppers or anybody else being able to feed that many mouths—well, that qualifies as a miracle as far as I'm concerned.

The second miracle is even more stunning. It was amazing that Mama had eighteen children and even more amazing that she wanted to keep all of us. Keeping my nine sisters made sense, but we boys tried every thread of her patience most every day. If I had been in Mama's shoes, I might not have been as gracious as she was.

Another miracle was that Daddy managed to keep us kids in shoes, at least most of the time. With fifteen of us living at home at once, that added up to a lot of shoes. It is not that shoes were compulsory where I was born. In Celina, Texas, barefoot children were practically the norm. Most families were poor like us, so bare feet made no difference to anybody. No one was embarrassed by them and no one felt judged.

Then Daddy found work in Plano. It was a larger town and not as rural as Celina. Things that were acceptable in Celina seemed out of place in Plano, not because the people were less good or caring, but because the culture was different.

When I showed up at school in my bare feet, I saw just how different it was. My first-grade teacher explained that going shoeless in school was not OK. Needless to say, my folks found me some shoes in a hurry. I still don't know whose they were or where they came from. I do know they solved the problem.

As simple as those shoes were, they meant a lot that day. Still bigger needs would arise in the months and years to come. Some were life-and-death-sized miracles; but whatever the size and shape, they always began with my parents' focus on God.

GOD AT THE CENTER

Daddy worked as hard as a man could work, and Mama did everything that needed doing at home. They gave all they had to give, and then gave some more. But in their doing, they always looked heavenward. They knew that raising their family would take more than earthly power and elbow grease. Someone would always be in need of something, and new challenges were sure to pop up.

The hallmark of my parents' lives was how they kept God at the center. They knew who held them and they called on Him regularly. What an excellent example they set for us! My siblings and I were like all children; we watched how our parents lived and applied the lesson to our own lives.

Trusting God was everything in our house, but it never meant kicking back. Daddy worked tirelessly. Each day he left the house at sunup. Each evening he returned as daylight faded, so covered with soil and debris that the whites of his eyes were the only part of him we could see.

No doubt Daddy drew strength from the Scriptures. I know he read his Bible every day. He was an honorable man who honored others. He was soft-spoken and never said a bad word about anyone, not even when people seemed to deserve it. Daddy was a principled man who loved his family and demanded respect. He was strict, but not hard. He enjoyed laughter and singing, and he was always aware of our needs.

When I was five, Mama asked my baby brother, Paul, and me to take lunch to Daddy in the field where he and others had been gathering wheat in the hot sun. When we reached the field, the three of us sat down to eat on the shady side of a truck with the other laborers. It was clear that the other men were accustomed to coarse conversation. They continued swearing without a second thought about us kids.

That did not sit well with Daddy. He didn't judge the men, but he did take action. He took us and our lunch to the opposite end of the truck. I was struck by how he handled the situation. It was the first time in my life that I understood the depth of Daddy's commitment to doing the right thing.

Moving us to the other side of the truck was a simple response, but it meant Daddy would get no relief from the sun until nightfall. For a man laboring long and hard in the Texas heat, it was a sacrifice. But Daddy would not have it any other way. Shielding Paul and me from vulgarity was more important to him than sitting in the shade. It was the right thing to do, and Daddy never hesitated to do what was right.

Mama was his perfect match. She read her Bible daily and kept her eyes on Jesus. He was her best friend, and everyone knew it. She never put on religious airs. No one would have called her a Holy Roller or a Bible thumper.

Her relationship with Jesus went much deeper than appearances and rules. Mama's life was an ongoing conversation with God. No matter what happened or how hard things got, she stayed close to Him.

We knew Jesus was Mama's best friend, but He was also her Lord. She expected us to see Him that way too. Even as my siblings and I became adults, Mama would speak up if we got crosswise of Him. She did not need many words; seven got her point across: "That's not what Jesus expects from you," Mama would say.

Our mother spoke her mind and loved us too much to sugarcoat the truth. Whether by word or deed she always made Jesus real to us. Never letting up, Mama prayed for us till she died at the age of eighty-five.

BORN AGAIN AT LEBANON BAPTIST

When I was seven, we moved to Frisco, Texas, a sharecropping town. No one there minded when we dragged our beds onto the porch in summertime. We had no air-conditioning, and the temperatures barely budged at night. Sleeping outside gave us much-needed relief from the oppressive Texas heat.

I have fond memories of Frisco and of our little wood-framed church there. Lebanon Baptist Church was a country congregation where everyone was family. Nobody had much in the way of material goods, but we always found a way to help one another. During a season when both Mama and Daddy were very sick, we kids were without parents for an extended period of time. Our church family made sure we were cared for. No one made a big deal about the sacrifice; everyone did his or her part quietly and with joy.

Not all the "warmth" at Lebanon Baptist was meant to give comfort. Pastor John Meyers was a sweat-soaked hellfire preacher with a wooden leg and an even stiffer message. His sermons were so strong that I perspired in my pew as profusely as he did in the pulpit. I doubt I was the only one who felt the flames of hell move closer when Pastor Meyers preached about sin and death. Yet as unforgettable as his fiery messages were, his sermons about God's love were the ones that eventually won my heart.

My good friend Jimmy Eaton and I talked often about getting saved. One Sunday when Pastor Meyers finished preaching, he gave the altar call. It wasn't the first invitation Jimmy and I had heard. Yet this time we looked at each other with a certain knowing that our day had come. I was eleven and Jimmy was around my age. As young as we were, we knew we would not live forever, and hell was not where we wanted to end up.

The fear of hell was only a piece of the puzzle for me. When I heard the altar call that day, I knew God was real and I wanted to spend eternity with Him. I believe Jimmy felt the same way.

So we elbowed each other, neither of us wanting to blaze the trail to the front. We bartered back and forth, each of us promising the other, "I'll go if you go." Finally, I took the lead, and Jimmy followed. Within minutes we had given our lives to Jesus Christ and received Him as our Savior and Lord.

What a memorable day it was! I had already seen God's goodness toward my family, but now I had my own relationship with Him. Deep inside I knew He would direct the rest of my life. There was nothing theological about my approach; theology was the furthest thing from my mind. I only knew that God loved me and would never leave me.

My relationship with Him grew from that moment forward, more steadily at some times than others. Whether I got it right or wrong on a given day, God remained faithful. He proved over and over again that He would never ever leave me. I knew in my heart that when I drew my last breath, I would head straight to heaven, and He would receive me with open arms.

For the time being, however, it felt good not to sweat when Pastor Meyers preached hellfire on Sunday mornings.

BOYHOOD THOUGHTS ABOUT DYING

Two years or so before I gave my heart to Christ, an experience with sudden death shook me. It happened during Sunday morning service as Eva Bryant led the congregation in song. Eva had a great voice. In fact, it was good enough to keep her brother Paul awake on the first row. Unfortunately Eva could not keep him awake during Sunday sermons. Paul was well known for napping during those.

This particular Sunday service had started out like any other. Paul sat in his usual seat on the first row to the left of the podium. Eva began the worship, and the congregation chimed in. Then, midway through a song, a most unexpected drama unfolded.

Eva's beautiful voice turned bloodcurdling as she screamed, "Paul!" and threw her songbook clear across the sanctuary.

Everyone turned to look. Paul was neither awake nor asleep. He was dead of a heart attack. Shock gripped my soul. I could not grasp the suddenness and finality of what had occurred. One thing I knew: if God could take a man home in the middle of Sunday service, He could take anybody home at any time.

Little did I know that in just a few years, I would see sudden death up close.

REAL-LIFE DEATH SENTENCE

It's a good thing my dad had a strong work ethic, because farming is not for those prone to laziness. Besides being physically demanding, farming is also stressful. Crops and weather have minds of their own. They demand attention regardless of how you feel or what is on your agenda. Daddy was fine with that. Regardless of weather, fatigue, or worries, he showed up to work.

On a certain fall morning that seemed like any other, my dad headed out for a day of plowing. In a mundane moment when we least expected our lives to change, they were turned inside out. Daddy suffered a heart attack so massive it could have finished him off on the spot.

It didn't. Nevertheless, doctors had no hope he would recover. They made their fears clear to Mama from the outset: not only were Daddy's farming days behind him, but the days of his life were numbered. The strong, able-bodied man she loved had a death sentence hanging over him.

Doctors had every medical reason to be pessimistic. My mother, however, refused to accept their prognostications. She did what she always did: she looked to Jesus. Mama respected the doctors and their expertise, but her faith was in her Lord.

She would need every bit of that faith for what was ahead. Daddy survived the heart attack but was too sick to leave the hospital. Months later, when his condition still had not improved, his doctors sent him home to die.

KEEPING THE FAITH

Mama knew why Daddy had been released, yet she remained steadfast. As long as he had breath, she would take care of him. She was as devoted to prayer as she was to attending to his physical needs. Although Daddy had become very frail and showed no significant signs of recovery, Mama believed he would recover.

Despite her vigilance, Daddy took an ominous turn for the worse one night. Dr. Charlie recognized all too well the signals Daddy's body was sending. He told my dad in no uncertain terms: "Lee Roy, you'll not live through the night."

Dad understood what Dr. Charlie was saying, but he rebuked him anyhow. "Doc, I will tell you when I am ready to die, and tonight is not the night."

Dr. Charlie fared no better getting Mama to believe him. In all the earnestness he could muster, he warned, "Bessie, Bud's not going to make it through the night."

Mama would have none of it. With pure grit and the courage of her convictions, she replied, "If you think Bud's going to die, then you don't know my Jesus!"

It was not the first time Mama had spoken frankly to a doctor. Many years earlier my oldest sister, Opal Lee, was near death. She was just a baby at the time and nobody knew what was wrong with her, at least not at first. By the time doctors diagnosed the problem, Opal Lee's appendix had ruptured and gangrene set in. Her condition was too far gone to be treatable, so doctors sent her home to die.

Mama scooped up her little girl and admonished the doctors: "If you think this baby is going to die, you don't know my Jesus."

Both Mama and the doctors were right: Opal Lee died—at the age of seventy-nine!

MY SOLEMN PRAYER

Despite Daddy's terrible condition, the year's final wheat crop needed harvesting. Fortunately my siblings and I were experienced. As a sharecropper Daddy never needed to hire outside help; he just took us along whenever he needed extra hands in the field.

The training did us good. We not only learned farming, but we also learned to work together and help others. Each of us (brothers and sisters alike) had our own row to hoe, down one end and up the other. After each one we would pause long enough to gulp water from the bucket, take a breath, and carry on.

Because I was younger and smaller than all but one of my siblings, I often lagged behind. My sister Fayola always kept an eye on me and made sure I wasn't left behind. She was my "mother hen." Sometimes she sacrificed her water break to look after me. In fact, none of my older siblings would take their breaks without me.

That is how Daddy taught us to live. It was never about "me, myself, and I," but about "us" and how we could serve one another. Now that Daddy was unable to work, we knew what to do. All of us boys pitched in financially, not only by working the fields, but also by taking other jobs after school.

With my younger brother I herded cattle for a neighbor. Starting around age thirteen, I regularly took on full-time jobs after school. One was a ranching job. In order to get there quickly after classes, I rode a motorcycle. Like my siblings, I did whatever was necessary to keep the family going—but only after promising my parents that I would finish my schooling as well.

Now with the wheat crop ready and Daddy laid up, we needed all the help we could get. So my uncle brought up his combines and worked with us to gather the crop.

While we took in the harvest, my grandmother heard the awful news from Dr. Charlie: her son was going to die. Beset by grief, she came out to the field and told us what was about to happen.

My heart sank fast and hard. I climbed into the wheat truck and pounded the piles of grain with my fists. I cried out to God, "It's not fair! I want Daddy to see my children. I want him to hold my kids. Please, God, let Daddy live till then."

DEATH UP CLOSE

Mama was upset with Grandma for spreading the bad news while we were out in the field. Yet it was not as though anyone was surprised. The doctors had made Daddy's prognosis clear from the beginning. We had lived with uneasiness and uncertainty ever since. We expected Daddy's death on the one hand and struggled to deny it on the other.

Despite months of imagining the worst, my grandmother's words shook me. Once inside the house I claimed the end of the couch beside my father's recliner and listened as my mother and sisters talked about what to do next. I watched as they applied cold cloths to Daddy's head. I wondered what to expect and wished it would not happen. The closest I'd ever been to death was when Paul Bryant died in church. Not even the death of a grandparent had touched me, because my mother's parents died before I was born.

My father's death would be a first for me—one I never

wanted to face. Yet it seemed inevitable now. Cold cloths were not helping; his condition only grew worse. Doctors could offer neither help nor hope. Disease had run its course, and my father's end seemed imminent.

I'd often thought about the impact Daddy's death would have, and about what our lives would be like without him. That hot summer evening my fears materialized. Mama was the first to notice something going wrong. She ran to Daddy's side, hoping against hope. She saw what we all dreaded: his breathing and heart had stopped.

Daddy's head tilted back, his eyes still open. Mama shouted, "Hurry! Get another cold cloth and wipe his face!"

It was no use. Daddy was gone, and Mama knew it. She pulled his body close to hers. In that surreal moment Daddy seemed to look straight at me. I could not take my eyes off him. Soon I realized that his eyes were open, but not seeing. Instead, they were fixed in death. Awestruck, speechless, and unable to cry, I had only one thought in my mind: "This is it."

The day I feared had arrived.

Mama knew Daddy was dead, yet she refused to surrender. Still clutching his body tightly, she looked up toward heaven and prayed the simplest of prayers: "Jesus, help us!"

Immediately she repeated herself: "Jesus, help us!"

In that instant Daddy revived. With what sounded like a deep, almost gulping breath, he stirred and blinked his eyes. Mama had prayed him back to life!

It was just as Hebrews 11:35 says: "Women received back their dead, raised to life again." Daddy's health was not instantaneously restored, but he was alive and our family was intact. Day by day his strength grew. Still, Daddy never returned to work. He was old enough to retire and had weathered the demands of farming long enough.

Daddy's "death sentence" had been revoked, and he lived another thirty years! Today, I have photos of him with all of my children. My pleas in the wheat truck were answered.

THE POSSE

For as long as I can remember, Mama was a strong pray-er, and so were my sisters. The apples did not fall far from the tree.

In 1950, my sisters rose to the occasion when my brother Morris Junior[1] was called up to fight in the Korean War. Most of the girls were still living at home when the conflict began. They sensed a calling to pray for Morris Junior's protection and agreed to do it regularly. Their persistence was well known—so much so that they became known as the Posse.

The Posse took many prayer cues from Morris Junior's letters home. They did a great job of praying through every item until he was safe, sound, and out of the war zone. Although their original mission was accomplished, the Posse never disbanded. They continued praying for decades to come! Whenever a situation arose or someone had a need, the Posse prayed. Their track record was so good that they would one day be asked to refrain from prayer.

It was a very special request and they honored it.

Mama and Daddy enjoyed decades together after he returned from death. By the time he reached the ripe age of ninety-one, Mama was already in heaven and Daddy had his share of health problems. Both had weathered numerous emergencies and hospital stays in their latter years. Now Daddy faced a new one.

At seven-thirty in the morning my wife, Debbie, and I received a call from the hospital. Daddy had been admitted and was doing poorly. We'd received calls like this before. Always, we wondered whether it would prove to be the last one; and always, we went straight to Daddy's side.

This time we reached him in an hour's time. The whole family had been notified, and his room quickly filled up with children and grandchildren. By late morning all my siblings had arrived except for one—my brother Hack, who lived in Oklahoma. Hack was on his way and would arrive soon.

Needless to say, a hospital room was a tight squeeze for the Vest clan. We were used to being crammed into close quarters, but not this close. In her later years Mama had twenty to thirty grandkids over to the house every Sunday for dinner. Christmas dinner was another story: the family eventually got so big we had to rent a school gymnasium to accommodate upwards of one hundred fifty people.

With Daddy's hospital room packed, my sister Murlene informed me of his special request to the Posse. At his urging, they promised not to pray for his recovery. Daddy knew how effective their prayers were, and he did not want to remain earthbound. He wanted to be released from his body and delivered to his eternal home. As much as he loved us, he was ready to be with his Lord in heaven.

The only other request Daddy made was the same one Mama shared before she passed on: it was for the family to stay together. Like Mama, Daddy loved his family and wanted us to remain tightly knit. With all thankfulness I can say that we remain close to this day.

DADDY'S HOMEGOING

Daddy did not have the look of a man on death's doorstep. He was completely coherent as he visited with everyone, including Hack, who arrived sometime before noon.

Surrounded by all eighteen of his children, and satisfied that he'd said all he needed to say, Daddy smiled really big and said, "Praise the Lord! Come on! Praise the Lord! Come on!" As he spoke he motioned with his hand as though directing someone to come toward him. He was not looking at any of us; he was looking beyond us and over our heads. I believe Daddy saw the angels Jesus had sent to bring him home.

In that moment I heard God's voice in a way I'd never heard it in forty-three years on planet Earth. It was audible—not outside where everyone could hear Him, but inside where I heard every syllable as plain as day. His message was clear: "It's time," He said. "Call the family in. I have something I want you to say."

"Lord," I begged, "please ask my brother Paul to do it. He's more spiritual than I am."

My heavenly Father responded in a way He knew I would understand. He spoke exactly the way Daddy did whenever I wavered. "Now!" was all He said.

I called in any who had stepped out into the hall. Then I shared what God had given me to say: "Mama and Daddy prayed that their kids would grow up to love the Lord, be saved, and join them in heaven someday. They did not ask that we would be popular or wealthy, but saved. Their desire has always been for us to remain together as a family, all of us Christians."

Then I shared what God revealed: "It's time for Daddy to go and be with the Lord."

Nobody protested. God's peace had settled over each of us, and we were content with His plan. With a short prayer, I gave thanks for the wonderful father we had been blessed to know and love. I ended the prayer saying, "Lord, we now commit Daddy's spirit back to You."

Then I turned to the family and said, "We need to give Daddy some traveling music."

Murlene replied instantly. "We should sing 'Amazing Grace.'"

Everyone sang—and what a sound it was! During the first verse, Daddy looked us in the eye, one by one, deliberately and with purpose. He was going to leave this earth expressing his devotion in a way so personal and filled with love that there would be nothing left to do but turn and meet Jesus face-to-face.

As the verse ended, Daddy looked into one last pair of eyes and drew his final breath. Immersed in peace, he left us. One last time his eyes remained open...his gaze fixed.

The room broke out with shouts of praise. "Thank You, Jesus! Thank You, Jesus! Thank You, Jesus!" was all I heard.

Then Hack closed Daddy's eyes and wished for just a moment that God would let us keep him another thirty years. It was fitting for Hack to say this. He had prayed for Daddy's recovery thirty years prior.

Despite his quiet wish, Hack wasn't sorrowful. None of us were. We were thrilled to see our daddy ushered into heaven. We knew that he was in a far better place— the place he longed to be! There was no cause for sadness or fear of death. We had witnessed something more beautiful than words could describe. What we saw kindled the greatest hope of all: the promise of heaven.

Mama wasn't there to pray Daddy back that day. I believe she prayed him home instead.

Chapter 3

LIFE in the FAST LANE

God has said, "Never will I leave you;
never will I forsake you."
HEBREWS 13:5

OMEWHERE ALONG THE line came the idea that Christians never sin. If only that were true! I don't speak as a "model Christian" or a Bible teacher, but as a Christ-follower who has sinned more than once. The truth is that only Jesus Christ was sinless. Knowing that helps me to get past my failures and keep on trusting Him.

Even after all He has done for me, I will never be in His league where sin is concerned. I am forgiven, but I am not sinless. What I am is grateful, eternally grateful, that despite my failings, He has never chased me off, shut me down, or stopped loving me. With all my flaws I'm still His. That is amazing!

I am 100 percent human. Anyone who knows me can tell you that! No one knows it better than God and I. His love helps me to navigate and understand His way of living. Yet even when I try my best, I eventually miss the mark somewhere.

You can probably say amen to that. We all face challenges and we all want to kick ourselves at times. It's nothing new. All the way back in God's perfect garden Adam and Eve probably kicked themselves too. They had it all. Life was beautiful, yet sin tripped them up. The whole world is still dealing with that one.

Every revered "hero" of the Bible was as imperfect as Adam, Eve, you, and me. I suppose that is why, these centuries later, their stories ring true. On the one hand they followed God with every fiber of their being. Their mountaintop experiences stir our hopes. Yet they also lived through messy trials. More than once they hit the wall. No wonder they are cheering us on from heaven! (See Hebrews 12:1.)

Noah is a perfect example of what I mean. He accomplished an amazing feat. He heard God's voice and prepared for a flood before rain had been seen on the earth. He obeyed God knowing his neighbors would call him a crackpot. The impact of his obedience was massive—the preservation of humankind and the animal kingdom!

You would think a guy as in tune to God as Noah would have it all together. But that is just the point. Noah was as imperfect as the rest of us. Temptation got to him like it can get to anyone. After the flood receded and Noah's mission was complete, his sons found him passed out, drunk and naked.

He was not the only one who stumbled. Abraham's story is similar. He tenaciously followed God before he had a clue where it would lead. He uprooted his family and they lived as nomads. He believed God's promise that he would have a son—and not only a son, but also descendants as numerous as the stars in the sky. Imagine believing all that knowing you and your wife are both over the hill and still childless!

That is some kind of faith. Yet Abraham also went weak at the knees and twice put his wife at terrible risk. To avoid the wrath of heathen kings, he told them she was his sister. They wanted her and assumed they could have her. I can only imagine how she felt—or how my own wife would feel if I pulled a stunt like that!

Abraham was not the last Bible hero to fall short. David, God's chosen king, committed adultery and then upped the ante by arranging a murder. And Peter, the man whose brilliant revelation got Jesus's attention (Matt. 16:17), denied the Savior in His darkest hour, not once but three times!

I can so relate to these men's weaknesses. Yet I honor them as Scripture does, not because they behaved perfectly, but because they trusted God and followed Him even when failure dogged them.

These men give me hope. They show me that my humanness does not disqualify me from being passionately loved by God. He is never shocked by my failures. He saw them coming before I was conceived. That's why Jesus went to the cross in the first place. I needed redemption. We all do. None of us can redeem ourselves.

Even when I failed Him, God never discarded me. The depth of His love and commitment is truly mind-blowing.

He prepared a solution for my failures thousands of years before I was born. If that doesn't beat all, I don't know what does.

SIDETRACKED BY SIN

Even after the upbringing my parents provided, I chose a rocky road for a period of time. I don't share it because I'm proud of it, but because it taught me so much about myself and about God.

When I was twenty, I got married. Soon my wife and I were blessed with a precious son, Rowdy. Our marriage did not go well; by the time Rowdy was seven, we were divorced, and my season of drifting was well under way.

As a thirty-year-old divorcé my heart hardened. I decided that marriage was not for me—period. I'd been there, done that, and had no intention of going there again. My sour attitude was not about my wife; it was about me and my issues. The marriage did not work out and I had no idea how to fix it. As far as I could tell, divorce was my best and only option.

I regretted that Rowdy had to live with the divorce too. Nevertheless, I tried to make the most of my single status. Because of my upbringing and my faith, there were limitations as to how far afield I was willing to go. Yet I did some things that weren't right. It was not that I didn't know better; I did. My downward slide was my choice, and I knew it.

Even in the midst of my mess, God did not walk away from me. In fact, He reached out, giving me countless nudges to change my ways. He would speak to me on the inside and say, "You don't need to be doing this, Freddy. You don't have to take this road."

He was so faithful! I knew His voice, and I knew better than to ignore it. Yet I brushed Him aside, at least for a time. I did not notice the callus that was growing over my heart. The more I withdrew from Him, the thicker it got, and the smaller His voice seemed to be. At times I felt twinges of remorse, but not enough to change my ways. I was having fun, and I wanted to have even more.

Despite my stubbornness and wandering, I never denied Jesus. He was still my Savior; I was certain of that. I kept looking to Him and always knew deep down that He cared.

In all the craziness I continued to pray...and He still listened.

As challenging as my twenties were, they also brought the fulfillment of two cherished dreams. The most important one was becoming a father. The second was becoming a rodeo cowboy.

The rodeo dream came out of thin air when I was just nine or ten years old. It started on a spring morning in Frisco, when Mama said my Uncle Bill was coming for a visit. He was Mama's baby brother and lived in Okmulgee, Oklahoma. Because it was a long drive from Frisco, we rarely saw him.

Uncle Bill was striking in every way. He had black curly hair and was a very big man—six foot six and two hundred forty pounds, with big, broad shoulders to match his extra-long frame. This was not unusual on Mama's side of the family. Except for Mama, everyone was extra tall, including her sisters. One of the girls stood an inch over six feet and was...well...let's just say she was solidly built.

Uncle Bill was a friendly man who loved a good joke. He loved kids too. He was the kind of person who found his way into your heart and made you feel better for knowing him. He was a real "people person." In all truth, he could have charmed a rattlesnake as easily as he did us.

By trade Uncle Bill was a pipefitter who worked contract jobs all over the country. But his real love was calf roping. He did that all around the country too. And did he ever look the part! When he showed up that spring morning he was 100 percent cowboy. I can still see his pointy-toed boots, cowboy hat, Texas-sized smile, and trophy belt buckle.

I also remember how impressed I was when he had to crouch just to come in the front door. Once inside Uncle Bill removed his hat, bent over again, and gave Mama a big hug. As big as he was, I could see the love and respect he had for her. The feeling was mutual. The tenderness between them stuck in my mind. So did the idea of being a cowboy.

A HORSE AND A HAT

As though the sight of him had not inspired me enough, Uncle Bill asked me to take care of his horse for a couple of weeks while he traveled to Houston. The horse had a cut on its hoof and needed some extra care. I was taken aback by the request and felt proud to be asked. Uncle Bill made me feel like a somebody that day!

Two weeks later he returned to find his horse in better shape than the day he left for Houston. I'd looked after the horse's hoof just like he asked. He was pleased with the outcome and gave me some money. I'd have done it all for free, but he insisted. How much money he gave me, I don't remember. Nor did I really care. It had never been about the money as far as I was concerned.

Uncle Bill seemed to understand what all this meant to me. He reached into the back of his car and pulled out a cowboy hat he had probably worn for three or four years. It was nicely broken in. To me it was the ultimate. My eyes must have been as big as saucers; I guess Uncle Bill pretended not to notice. "Would you like to have this?" he asked.

"Oh man! You know it!" was all I could say.

Uncle Bill gave me the hat. It was so big it flopped down over my ears. That made no difference to me. I was going to wear the hat one way or another. So I stuffed it with enough newspaper to help it stay put. In retrospect it probably looked peculiar, but it was the genuine article, and I loved wearing it.

Uncle Bill's visit was pivotal for me. It birthed a dream that changed the course of my life. After seeing him, I realized I wanted to be a cowboy. Uncle Bill realized it too. We both knew he couldn't stay around Frisco much; but while he was there, he showed me how to work toward my dream.

Again he walked to the back of his car. This time he opened the trunk and grabbed a rope from his rope can. Then he set a five-gallon bucket on the ground and taught me how to rope it. Pretty soon I learned how to make the loop land over the top of the bucket.

Then Uncle Bill spoke cowboy to cowboy and said exactly what I needed to hear: "Freddy, you just keep practicing, and you'll be a calf roper."

His words settled deep in my heart. I practiced so much that I wore out the rope. For years practicing was the best I could do. I was still young; breaking into rodeo would take time and money. Years would pass before my opportunity came. Until then the dream kept stirring inside me.

When I was twenty-five years old, I bought a saddle and the rest of the gear I needed. My career in calf roping had officially begun, but the dream went all the way back to the spring day when Uncle Bill towered in our doorway in Frisco, Texas.

The impression Uncle Bill made was indelible. I loved the man and wanted to be the kind of cowboy he was. It would be years before I understood everything that would entail. Not all of it would be good for me in the long run. Looking back, I would have done well not to follow his pattern as closely as I did.

To whatever degree I veered from the straight and narrow, it wasn't because I lacked a good foundation. Daddy showed me how a man should live. Mama taught me about Jesus and how to honor Him with my life.

They laid out clear boundaries about what was and was not OK.

For example, by the time I was old enough to understand what alcohol was, I knew drinking was not OK with Mama. She did not want any of her kids involved with the stuff, and I knew it. So did my brother Morris Junior. After he returned from Korea, Mama read me one of his wartime letters. In it he shared a story that showed just how solid our upbringing was.

Morris Junior explained how scarce water had been during the war. At the time of his letter, the only water he and his comrades could find was in a mud hole. The other soldiers felt fortunate to have an alternative: an ample supply of canned beer, which they gladly drank instead.

Even with the pressures of war, Morris Junior would not drink beer. That left him only one option: to boil the slop from the mud hole and drink it. Even after boiling, I doubt it was pleasant to drink. But Morris Junior made it work. The values he learned at home stuck with him, even when he had the "perfect excuse" to set them aside.

All of us had the same good pattern to follow—the one our parents lived by. Overall I would say we followed it pretty well. Speaking for myself, however, there were plenty of challenges and a fair number of missteps.

The wavering began during my first marriage and escalated after my divorce. After long hours at the rodeo I always headed straight for the bar, where I grabbed a drink and a stool. It seemed like the best place in the world to unwind after roping calves. I could make conversation with pretty young ladies and shoot the breeze with my friends, often until closing time. Then I would either go out for breakfast or go home.

Before long I was running in the same circles as Uncle Bill. I thought it was all fun, but he knew the ups and downs better than anyone my age could. Before he died, he offered me some advice, through another uncle of mine: "Son, roping, chasing women, and drinking don't mix. You can drink when you get old."

Uncle Bill knew what he was talking about. I appreciated his caring enough to share a piece of his mind. Still, I found it interesting that he never urged me to quit roping or chasing women.

LIVING THE LIFE

My nephew Rick and I spent a lot of time together, especially during days at the rodeo and nights at the bar. We lived it up, always with a sense of humor and never meaning to hurt anyone.

We were good natured, but we were mischievous too. Early one morning at about two we closed down the bar like we usually did and went to a place called Jo-Jo's for breakfast. The restaurant was packed. At that hour you would expect a lively atmosphere, but everyone looked down in the dumps.

I turned to Rick and said, "Not a single person in this place is smiling."

My wheels were turning. I didn't say much, but I told

Rick, "Give me about five minutes. Then go to the front door."

Rick knew me well enough to know what was coming. He gave me a skeptical look and said, "Freddy, this is a restaurant."

His warning did not faze me. I went out to my trailer, saddled up, and rode my horse to the front door and then into Jo-Jo's. The diners' sour faces disappeared and laughter filled the room. To my delight and the owner's dismay, everyone applauded.

Without a hint of a smile, the owner exclaimed, "You cannot do this!"

I could not resist the irony of his statement, and replied, "I don't know, but I think I just did it."

That prank started a tradition for Rick and me. We looked to outdo ourselves from that point on. One night I rode my horse into the Safeway supermarket that was next to the saloon. It was late, so there were only a few people in the store. Still, it was quite a scene—a hilarious one, no doubt, especially because the floor had just been waxed to a slick finish. My horse slipped and slid every step of the way.

Finally I got him back outside and told Rick to hold him still for a second. Rick must have known he was in for something, and he was. What I did next was dangerous; I would advise any human being not to do it: I climbed into a shopping cart behind the horse and took hold of his tail. With all seventy-three inches and two hundred pounds of me stuffed inside the cart, I let the horse pull me through the parking lot, which happened to slope downward.

When the horse broke into a trot, I knew I was in trouble. The combination of speed and a downward slope sent the cart hurtling forward at a treacherous rate. I had to let go of the horse and pray that I could pry myself out of the cart in time.

You can probably imagine what happened next: the cart hit the curb and catapulted me through a hedgerow! I landed in the lawn of a neighboring restaurant where a cook who had emigrated from Asia stood smoking a cigarette.

When I somersaulted into his line of sight, he applauded and said, "You crazy Americans! Only in America!"

As funny as the scene was, I could have gotten myself and somebody else killed that night. None of that entered my mind. I can only thank God for the way He watched over Rick and me. It is true that we were good-natured pranksters, but we did get carried away.

We never wanted to hurt anybody, and we never did…except once.

One night as I walked beside the bar counter, I saw a guy roughing up a young woman. He had pinned her arm behind her and was pinching her hard. The woman did not appreciate his advances; it was clear that he was hurting her.

The guy had no business treating a lady that way, so I spoke up. "Hey fella," I said, "that's not good."

He didn't appreciate my input, and snapped back, "You want some of this?"

There was not much left to say at that point except, "Yeah I do. Let's take care of this outside."

He agreed and outside we went. With both testosterone and alcohol involved, there was no way it would end well. He got big and cocky, and I had watched too many John Wayne movies. I told him, "I'll give you a free shot. You just go ahead and hit me. It's on after that."

Not to be outdone, he said, "No. You take the free shot. Come on. Hit me."

As far as I was concerned, he had his chance, and he let it get away. I took him up on the free shot, and the fight was definitely on. It continued for a good five or ten minutes. When I pinned him on the ground and put my hands around his throat, he forced out three words: "I...can't...breathe."

In my best John Wayne style I wisecracked, "You're not supposed to."

Rick sized up the situation and said, "Let him go, Freddy. He's had enough."

Rick was right. The guy was hurting, and there was no chance he would come back for more. So I let him go. When I turned to go back inside, I realized that from the waist up I was wearing nothing but a collar and two cuffs. The rest of my shirt was gone.

The bartender was kind enough to come outside with a T-shirt that advertised the bar. He appreciated my intervening on behalf of the young woman. As a bartender, he wasn't in a position to take on the bully, but he was glad I had stepped in.

The bully never bothered that woman again. For that I was thankful.

The things I did as a young cowboy caused some people to question my belief in Christ. They had good reason to wonder, because my behavior didn't always line up with His example. To them I looked like a hopeless sinner or a hypocrite, or both.

Their judgment brings me back to something I said at the beginning of this chapter: many people believe that Christians never sin. When that is the standard, you almost have to believe that wrongdoing disqualifies wrongdoers from salvation.

Yet even when my conduct was off base, God never disqualified me. Instead of removing His love and kicking me to the curb, He reached out, even when He knew I would reject His invitations. He honored my free will and allowed me to go places He did not want me to go. He knew it would get messy and even painful. He did not choose that for me, but He used it—all of it. One of the biggest things He taught me was not to judge others but to love them.

Lots of people disliked the path I was on years ago. Some wrote me off. God never did. He allowed me to get into situations that only He could get me out of. He reached me where I was and showed me a better way.

He never twisted my arm—but He did get my attention.

~~Chapter 4~~

RUNNING STRAIGHT
BACK to GOD

*"For I know the plans I have for you," declares
the LORD, "plans to prosper you and not to harm
you, plans to give you hope and a future."*
JEREMIAH 29:11

WHEN YOUR LIFE ends, there is no time for
do-overs—especially when your death comes
the way mine did. In my rodeo and partying
days, eternity was not the uppermost thought in my
mind. I was like a calf stalled in the chute and needing
some kind of push back toward God's best.

Like I said, I never denied Him or stopped praying,
but I liked the chute I was in. I was making money and
having what I thought was a lot of fun. The trouble was
that the direction I was headed would not end well or be
satisfying for long.

God knew that and He knew exactly what it would
take for me to change. The "push" came in an unexpected
package: a five-foot-three-inch nurse who worked with a
gal my nephew Rick was dating at the time.

Rick said, "You need to meet this girl."

At first I resisted. "Oh man," I thought, "here we go."

My life was about the rodeo and about staying single. I'd also gone into the home-building business and had done some acting. My agent got me work as an extra at first. Later I won bit roles on the hit shows *Dallas* and *Walker, Texas Ranger*. I also got a crack at the movies in the prequel, *Dallas: The Early Years*.

Acting isn't rodeo. In calf roping the clock is everything. In acting, it is more "hurry up and wait" than hurry up and win. I remember standing around for a dozen hours waiting to film a fifteen-second sequence. The down time seemed endless, but the pay was worth it. A half day of acting could earn me a month's wages anywhere else.

My life wasn't perfect. But it wasn't boring, either. Frankly I was OK with the status quo, and a blind date was the furthest thing from my mind. I had no idea that God was behind this one, yet I agreed to go. No doubt I thought I could enjoy an evening out without risking my standing as an unattached man. Had I realized who was behind the setup, I would have known better, and my single life would have flashed before me.

BLIND DATE EYE-OPENER

When date night came, my tune started to change. There was Debbie—blonde, blue-eyed, smiling, as cute as a button with a sweet personality to match. She definitely got my attention. Not only was she attractive, but she also had a sense of where she was headed in life. She was fresh out of nursing school and working in an operating room. It was a career path that took some tenacity.

After a few minutes of conversation my defenses melted, and I turned on the charm. Knowing it would get her attention, I stared up at the ceiling for a while. She asked, "What are you looking for?"

I unloaded what I admit was a very cheesy line. "There must be a hole up there," I said, "because an angel just fell from heaven."

Uncle Bill would have been proud. It wasn't the best line in the world, but it worked. Debbie eventually admitted thinking, "Yeah, right, cowboy. Can't you do better than that?"

We danced and talked and had a lot of fun that night. Debbie could have been out dining with a doctor, but she wasn't; she was out dancing with me. I didn't know that she had vowed never to marry a doctor. In fact, she had already told a friend that she wanted to marry a country boy from a big family. Debbie was an only child and had always longed for a big family. She liked that I came from one.

She did not seem to mind that I was a cowboy either. When the night was over we exchanged phone numbers. It would be two weeks before I dared to call her.

When I finally took the plunge, Debbie agreed to go out with me. I'd sworn myself to bachelorhood but continued to date Debbie. She was an easy person to be around— never demanding, judgmental, or critical. Spending time with her was unlike anything I had ever experienced. Before long I was hooked.

On our first date I asked Debbie, "Can you cook?"

Looking back, it was quite a question. She responded with some questions of her own. "Can I cook? Well, do you like Southern cooking?"

"It's my favorite," I replied.

"Then, yes. I can cook!"

Debbie had a more serious question for me. She held it until our second date. As point-blank as could be, she asked, "Are you a Christian?"

I knew what the right answer was, and I was glad it also happened to be the truth. "Yes, I'm a Christian," I replied. "I might not always act like it, but I am."

Without blinking, she said, "Well good, because if you weren't a Christian, we wouldn't have anywhere to go from here."

Debbie's mind was made up. I thank God for it, because her clarity was exactly what I needed. Before meeting her, I was headed in the wrong direction. Living footloose and fancy free was not what God had in mind. Through our relationship I began to see how off track my thinking was.

Debbie was my turning point back to God. I'd dated other women, but none of them affected me the way she did. None was important enough for me to change my ways. The night I met her started my journey back to where I belonged—living with God in the center of my life instead of on the sidelines.

Getting Serious

As much as I wanted to stay single, I did miss having someone special in my life. Until I met Debbie, I did not realize how much I missed it. She filled a space in my life that had never been filled before. The truth is that I didn't even realize the emptiness was there until she came along.

We spent lots of time with each other at the rodeo and with my son Rowdy. He was living with me at the time, and the three of us often barbecued together. I cannot imagine a better "fit" for us than Debbie. Not only did she embrace my son and have a good head on her shoulders, but she also knew how to have good, clean fun too. She even gave me some competition in the pranks department.

One starlit night not long before I proposed to Debbie, she and I, Rick, and my sister Trenna saddled up two horses for a two-mile ride into the center of town. The ladies took the reins; Rick sat behind Trenna, and I sat behind Debbie.

About a quarter mile from town Rick and I needed to relieve ourselves, so we dismounted and used a roadside bush for cover. We heard the girls giggling while they waited, but we had no idea what they were up to. By the time we finished, they had left for town without us.

Rick and I thought for sure they would come back and get us, but they didn't. Fortunately my folks' house was right on the outskirts of town. Rowdy had his Honda 50 mini bike stored there, so Rick and I got it out and cranked it up. He jumped on the front and I got on behind him. It wasn't an optimal ride; the bike was just big enough for one youngster to ride.

We were no doubt a sight as we pulled into the square in front of the gazebo that marked the center of town. Everyone hooted and hollered, including Debbie and Trenna, who were clearly enjoying the joke. Then, as I stood with my guard down and my back to the gazebo, I heard the sound of a horse's hooves. Debbie was riding my horse straight into the middle of the gazebo—which was not meant for horses!

What she was riding was no kid's pony. Flash was my roping horse, a snorty and skittish mount that was more than a handful. He would spook at just about anything. If a gum wrapper flew by, he'd blow up and duck off before you knew what happened. If he had done that in the gazebo (I still don't know why he didn't), we would have had to buy the thing.

Debbie showed some nerve pulling a stunt like that—enough to convince me that staying single was out of the question. I looked at her on that horse, turned to Rick, and said, "She's the one!"

Debbie and I married in 1985. I was hitting the rodeo hard at the time, and Debbie was the ideal travel companion. It was not unusual for us to make two or three rodeos in a single night. Squeezing in all of them wasn't easy. There was no time to stop for meals, so Debbie fed me as we rolled down the road. We kept up that pace until Colton was born. That was when we quit doing out-of-state rodeos and stuck with local ones here and there.

My acting career also tapered off. I still accepted some parts, but with a growing family, a budding building business, and the rodeo, I had more than enough on my plate.

Our priorities were taking shape, and details such as finding a church were important. One of the first things we did as a couple was to find a church. Debbie wasn't looking only to attend church; she wanted to be an active part of a church family. We chose Celina Baptist; it was the perfect pick for us. The people there were close, always caring, and never judgmental.

At the start of our marriage Debbie was more the spiritual leader than I was. I believe God used her determination to set our foundation right. Her passion for the Lord was visible to me and it affected me. I might not have cared what anyone else thought of me, but what Debbie thought mattered a lot. It was important to me not to disappoint her. I'm not saying I never disappointed her, because I did. But when I messed up, it hurt me to think that I'd let her down.

Once we were married, my ways changed. Bars and the wild life were out. There were plenty of fun things to do, but they were things Debbie and I did together. I never tired of being with her. Twenty-eight years later, I still haven't.

Debbie is one of a kind. In all these years she has never criticized or judged me—ever. She married me knowing I had a past, but she never made an issue of it. All she wanted was for us to head in the right direction together. She needed a spiritual relationship with the Lord; that was the foundation of her life. She needed me to have one too. As long as we were on the same page where He was concerned, our marriage would hold and our lives would fall into place.

Establishing God as our number one priority early on has paid off. Debbie and I are blessed to live with a strong sense of His loving care. It has gotten us through many long nights, difficult seasons, and almost insurmountable odds. I cannot thank Him enough for bringing us together—and for giving me enough sense to consent to that first date. Our almost thirty years of marriage have been sweeter than I could have imagined. Had I refused Rick's matchmaking, I might have missed it all.

To this day I cannot wait till evening when Debbie and I are home together. All seems right in the world when she is beside me; I am completely at ease when she is around. As gentle as she is, I know she would fight a bear for me. I'd do the same for her. She is the lifelong companion handpicked for me by God.

Not long ago Debbie and I had dinner with the kids. With all of them around the table, Debbie and I did not sit together. Believe me when I tell you, I felt it. It was so unnatural not to have her beside me.

We are rarely apart for a whole day. When we are apart, I spend half the time looking forward to our reunion. Never have I experienced the oneness I share with Debbie. Even if I had to, I don't think I could make it without her... unless, of course, I were in heaven.

BE CAREFUL WHAT YOU PRAY

Debbie and I have been blessed with a full life and a wonderful business. I started the company two years before we married. From the beginning it thrived, which of course was a great benefit to our family.

One morning many years ago I started my day in the usual way. Debbie's shift began early in the morning, so she was already at work. It was just me and the Lord. After reading my Bible, I prayed that God would make me a better Christian. I did not realize where that prayer would lead. I know now that God answers such prayers, whether I understand them or not. The apostle John explained it:

> This is the confidence we have in approaching God: that if we ask anything according to his will, he hears us. And if we know that he hears us—whatever we ask—we know that we have what we asked of him.
>
> —1 JOHN 5:14–15

God was definitely in favor of my being a better Christian. He also knew better than I did how to get me there. My hope, I suppose, was that I would become a better and better person each day, just for having asked. In the end I did grow spiritually, but God honored my request His way.

Be careful what you pray, but pray! God will do what you ask when you ask according to His will. He might not explain how He will do it, but count on Him to respond. What you can expect is a life lesson of one kind or another. If you are like me, you might not appreciate it at first, but you will in the long run!

Two years before my prayer Debbie and I sold our home and built one in Celina. Now, right after my prayer to become a better Christian, Debbie came home from work with a surprising statement: "Honey, I found where I want to live—Pilot Point."

I said, "Honey, no one lives in Pilot Point on purpose."

Don't misunderstand me. Pilot Point is a great place to live. It is thirteen miles from Celina—far enough for a fierce football rivalry that renders the two towns virtual archenemies. With my roots in Celina the thought of moving to Pilot Point was more than ironic.

The more important issue was Debbie's roots. She is from Mississippi, a state known for its beautiful trees. She loves foliage and longed for a property that reminded her of Mississippi. That would be hard to come by in Celina, but Pilot Point was a different story.

It seemed like an easy call to me, so I said, "OK. If that's where you want to live, then that's where we'll live!"

We bought a piece of property covered with trees and overlooking a lake. It was a dream and a perfect place to build. Before moving forward, we made some key decisions. First and foremost, we would build without incurring debt. Business was good, and so was cash flow. There was no need to take out building or property loans. With some patience and planning, we could sell the home in Celina and build the new one debt free. We would borrow a trailer to live in (not a mobile home, but a smaller camper-style trailer) and pay for building as we went along.

It seemed like a great plan. The Celina home sold at a profit and our business income had been steady. The new house would go up quickly, and we would be out of the trailer before we knew it. The camper gave us every incentive to stay on schedule; it was just fifteen or eighteen feet long and narrow too. Storage was a challenge, so we decided to build the barn first and put our stuff in it. With the barn up and our belongings safe, we would build the house on a strictly cash basis.

When we started the project, Colton was eighteen months old. By the time the house was about forty percent complete, the building industry nosedived. Our finances diminished, and prospects were virtually non-existent. Without money coming in, we had no choice but to suspend construction on our house and tough it out in the trailer. We had no good options: the Celina house was gone, and the new house was uninhabitable.

During that time our daughter, Leigh, was conceived. I can only imagine how uncomfortable the situation was for Debbie. Yet she never complained. While I did everything I knew to keep the business afloat, she encouraged me, saying, "Whatever we need to do, we'll do it."

The situation weighed heavily on me. We had a roof over our heads, but it was more than rustic living. The trailer was so cramped that I slept with a pole jammed against my back, and even Debbie had to crouch to take a shower. There was not room enough for our refrigerator, so we kept it outside the camper—not an ideal situation for a family, and especially not for a pregnant woman in search of a nighttime snack.

Everything was improvised. We had to hang our clothes in the barn, which presented a problem of its own. Dirt daubers (aka mud daubers) are wasps that love building mud nests in barns. You never have to wonder whether the bugs are around; they leave nasty stains everywhere. Needless to say, our clothes did not escape their markings.

Living in the camper was not that big a deal until it seemed like we would never get out of it. We were still living there when Debbie was seven months pregnant. The idea of bringing a newborn into that situation was beyond bad. How would four of us and a bassinet even fit?

It was a stressful period, to say the least. I was especially concerned for Debbie's comfort. Her mom was too. She lived in Colorado Springs and invited Debbie and Colton to visit for a week. It was a relief to know that they would have several days of normalcy.

I admit I was worried about Debbie going to Colorado. My fears grew when she called and said how wonderful it was to take a bath. I thought to myself, "My God, she's not coming home."

I would not have blamed her. But I also did not want to lose her, so I got creative. We had only a ceramic heater in the camper. The next day I bought a real heater and put it in the new house, which had some almost livable areas at that point. I dug out a piece of carpeting that was stored in the barn, and I laid it down to make at least one room cozy. My hope was that if Debbie came home—even if only to pick up her things and leave me—I'd have one last shot at winning her back.

Debbie did come back to find hot water, a real bath and bed, and our clothes stored in the house rather than in the barn. Her heart was warmed by the surprise. She let me know too by thanking me profusely. She was so excited about the new amenities that you would have thought she'd won the lottery.

It turned out that Debbie never thought of leaving me at all. Knowing the kind of woman she is, I should have known better than to think she would.

Our marriage weathered the storm, but our business and housing problems were far from over. Exhausted, I came to the end of myself and cried out to God: "Please tell me what I need to do!"

With our world turned upside down, I decided to buy the best lot I could find in a high-dollar Dallas suburb. Once again I thought the plan was foolproof. I knew the market, and I knew the kind of home that could get business humming again. So I planned a spec house with all the bells and whistles.

Both the house and location were perfect, but almost no one looked at either. Of the few who did, not one person made an offer. There was a lot riding on that house; unless it sold promptly, it would be an albatross, or worse.

Around that time a second opportunity presented itself. A major home-show concern, Kaleidoscope of Homes, asked to feature one of our models in their annual presentation of cutting-edge properties in the Dallas-Fort

Worth area. Because Kaleidoscope had a good reputation and always created a strong buzz, I knew that at least three thousand people would come through the show. With such high exposure the right house would surely sell. So we built the most beautiful home imaginable, and we landscaped it to the max.

Like everything else during that season, there seemed to be no such thing as a sure thing. We built a truly special home. Thousands of potential buyers viewed it. No one made an offer—no one.

I was at a loss. Everything I knew to do was done, and all of it had failed.

NOTHING LEFT BUT SURRENDER

Those months taught me a lot about my limitations as a human being. It was obvious that I could not fix everything, and as hard as I tried, nothing went according to plan.

Remember what I had prayed: I asked God to make me a better Christian. One area that apparently needed improvement was my tendency to lean on self. My "I've got to do something" mentality had to go. It was too much about me and too little about Him. Without realizing it, I had left little room for God to work.

By nature I was not a passive guy. My intentions were good; I just wanted things to work and everybody to be OK. Yet until I stepped aside and let God be God, I would ultimately disappoint everyone. So once again I cried out to Him, wondering what I was doing wrong and what I should be doing instead.

"Lord," I begged, "I'll do whatever kind of work You want me to do. If it's picking up cans on the side of the road, so be it. But I'm a simple man, and it's obvious that I'm not hearing You correctly. You're going to have to write it down for me to get it."

I had no real idea what that meant. Was I expecting a finger to write the answer on a wall somewhere? Or would God send a scribbled note in a bottle? I don't know. But in sheer desperation that is what I prayed.

I wasn't the only one praying. Our church prayed too. We needed every bit of prayer we could get! Already I had broken the news to Debbie that we were close to the end of our resources. We could pay interest on the two unsold homes for two more months and no more. "After that, we're done," I said.

We were much closer to the edge of financial destruction than I had ever imagined being. If God was trying to redirect my life, I was open to it. If folding the business was His plan, I'd accept that. All I asked was that we be able to pay our bills and exit the building business without owing anybody a red cent.

How He would accomplish all that was beyond me. I just knew it needed to happen—and fast!

Meanwhile we kept on keeping on. Nothing seemed to budge until a visitor popped in one day as I vacuumed the carpets at the first home. It was a realtor who asked, "Are you Freddy Vest?"

"Well, yes, ma'am. I am."

"I've been looking for you," she said. "I have a couple who wants to buy this house."

This was the best news I had heard in quite a while! "Well," I said, "I'm looking for you too!"

She was not kidding about the couple who wanted to buy the house. They really wanted it and wasted no time in staking their claim. We signed a contract to close in thirty days. It felt like the dam was beginning to break! Then came another gusher—we received an offer on the second house the very next week. We accepted the offer and set a closing date for the end of the month.

God had answered one of my prayers: the two sales would produce enough revenue to pay off all our bills. We would not make a profit on either sale, but that was OK. Leaving the building business with honor was what I wanted most. With everything paid off, we could move on to whatever God had in mind.

My larger question was answered next, in the most amazing way! At the closing of the first house, I signed the papers and moved on, spotting the buyer's name and quickly forgetting what it was. The realtor was handling the transaction, so names did not concern me.

Three weeks later, at the closing of the second home, I could not help but notice the buyer's last name: Jesus. It suddenly dawned on me that the last name of the party that bought the first house was Lord.

My jaw dropped! The buyers of what I thought would be my two final transactions in the building industry were Lord and Jesus. I had not yet figured out what God was saying in this, but I knew it was Him.

Later I showed Debbie the two contracts. "God is good," I said. "We are out of debt, and I can move on to whatever He wants me to do. Let's get my résumé going, and I'll start looking for work."

I still wasn't sure whether I was supposed to be a home builder or a can picker, but I knew God was in control. Anyone who could put together those two transactions with those names in that order could be trusted to lead me in the right direction. I was not the least bit worried or fearful of whatever changes He might make. If picking up cans along the road was my assignment, I would be the best can picker in Texas!

Almost immediately the phone rang. It was someone from California who knew someone from Mississippi who knew someone in Dallas who knew me. The caller needed to buy a house. In that moment the light went on in my heart, and I knew where God was leading. I told Debbie, "God wants me to build, and that's what I am going to do!"

Then I remembered my prayer; I had asked Him to write down the answer to my career question—and He had done it on those contracts! As if that weren't enough, He then confirmed His answer with twenty-six building contracts in eighteen months, and a steady stream of clients ever since.

From that day to this I have not built a single spec house. When deals seem tentative or delayed, I don't worry anymore. I know He's taking care of us, and I know He can be trusted.

And I don't mind living in Pilot Point one bit. I love it, and the trees are beautiful.

God's answer did not come wrapped the way I would have liked. Still, I can vouch for this: His answers are always best in the long run.

The hardship and confusion of that difficult season were tough to swallow. The process was long and humbling. It pressed me so hard that I questioned my calling in business. But more important than the discomfort was what I learned: (1) that I could not control everything, (2) that Jesus was my only hope, and (3) that He would always provide.

What beautiful lessons to learn. They changed my approach to life. As big as the change was, it was only an appetizer compared to what was ahead. The main course—the experience that revolutionized my heart and my mission—was still to come.

⚯ Chapter 5 ⚮

A SHORT RIDE to HEAVEN

*For God so loved the world that he gave his
one and only Son, that whoever believes in
him shall not perish but have eternal life.*
JOHN 3:16

WHEN I DIED at the rodeo in Graham, Texas, my friends stayed on the scene and fought for my life. I was not there with them; I had moved on. One moment I was sitting on my horse. The next moment I was somewhere else—somewhere beyond description.

Without travel, transport, angelic assistance, or the passage of time, I was with Jesus! It was exactly as I'd read in my Bible since childhood: I was absent from my body and "present with the Lord" (2 Cor. 5:8, NKJV).

And was it ever glorious! My body had failed, but I was free. Even better than free, I was alive—more completely alive than I had ever been. The change was instantaneous. There was no time to wonder where I was going. There was no distance to cover or ticket to punch. It had been punched when I answered the altar call with Jimmy decades earlier. Now my "transfer" was complete.

There were only the two of us—my Lord and me—in seamless union in the place He promised to His people. There were no thoughts of death, loss, or what might have been. Not even a twinge of regret or sorrow surfaced. My journey had ended in the best of all possible ways. I was utterly content in my eternal destination. In fact, I would not have traded it for anything.

JUST JESUS AND ME

No one explained where I was or whose company I was in. The knowing was as immediate as my arrival had been. I was with Jesus. It was not my mind that told me so; my mind had been left behind. It was still encased in the corpse that lay in the rodeo dust. I was free of mind and body. My reborn spirit was at liberty and at home in heaven, reunited with the One who gave me life and eternity with Him.

My abrupt departure did not leave me feeling the least bit slighted. I had no sense of unfinished business on Earth, no desire to go back and set anything right. There was nothing incomplete to gnaw at me. I was with Jesus, and nothing—nothing—else mattered. I was consumed in His love and His presence. What an overwhelming experience it was! If I tried for all eternity, I could not find words to describe the wonder of it.

There with Jesus, drenched in the perfect serenity that every human being longs to know, I had it all. The Garden of Eden could not have been better. The undisturbed peace Scripture describes was now mine. No effort was required to achieve it. It just was.

I had experienced a hint of it—the tiniest hint—when I was a small child. After playing hard in the Texas sun, I remember heading back inside, exhausted. Even with as many children as she had, Mama was there to comfort me. I would climb into her lap, where she would cradle me, stroke my tousled head, rock me, and sing a song saying how much she loved me. I knew I was in the safest, most loving place in the world, and I never wanted to leave.

Now with Jesus the experience was all that and more—infinitely more. His attention was undivided. It did not matter how many had just entered heaven; He and I were alone. The comfort He gave was more beautiful, more complete than even Mama could offer. It defied expression in words. It was thick with love and life—His love and His life, saturating heaven and all eternity. If I could have multiplied the childhood experience with my mother thousands of times over, it could not have touched this. As generous and devoted as Mama was, her love was barely a shadow of His.

It was as though Jesus had wrapped His arms around me and drawn me into Himself, where all that was not of Him dissolved. Every weight and care of the natural life was replaced with His love. No question lacked an answer. No fear could flourish. There were no needs at all and no demands to be met. Pressure was nonexistent.

If I could come close to explaining it in Texas terms, I would say there were no "I gotta dos" in heaven, not even one. It was so peaceful, so safe, so timeless—a resting place filled with the immeasurable love found in God's presence. It was home, and I was there with the One whose love for me is complete—so complete that He chose to die for me. There could be no better place, no better love, and no reason I would ever choose to leave.

There were no distractions in heaven. Nothing could (or would) strain my union with Jesus. I could not be separated from Him. Everything was Him and Him only. I experienced the oneness I'd read about in Scripture. It consumed me, and I loved it! I was with Him, but also in Him. Really, there was no difference between the two. His presence was all-encompassing. Nothing was outside of Him or beyond Him. "The fullness of Him . . . fills all in all" (Eph. 1:23, NKJV).

I understood His Lordship like never before. The magnitude of His greatness was self-evident. He and I were wholly connected, yet I was not His equal, and certainly not above Him. There was no such "place" as "above Him"! He was my exalted Lord and King. I was His subject and thrilled with the arrangement. It was the consummate relationship—a mere man invited to commune with the Creator of the universe! What more could I want?

No Words, No Thoughts

Jesus and I communicated without exchanging a word. There was no need of words—none at all. Communication did not happen outside me where words are heard. No senses were needed, no body language necessary. Our conversation (for lack of a better word) occurred within me, with perfect clarity. It was completely nonverbal. There was no doubt who was "speaking" to me; I never questioned what He was "saying." I knew it was my Lord. His message—His love—was unmistakable.

The exchange was seamless, from Spirit to spirit. Misunderstanding was not possible. The filter of my intellect was out of the way, left behind with my mouth and ears. All three remained in the shell that lay dead on the ground at the rodeo. Without them I "heard" my Lord perfectly. He conveyed the totality of His love in a way that my spirit received without thinking. Its supply was endless; it flowed unhindered. Like a branch drawing rich sap from the vine, I drank in the life imparted from His being. It was a kind of life I had never known.

Apart from the communication we shared, I had no thoughts. Heaven was not a place of thinking but of being. Memories of life on Earth never came up. Nor did I seek them. I thought of nothing, especially nothing of the world. Not even my own family came to mind. I guarantee you that if my mind had traveled to heaven with me, I would have longed for my family and been concerned for them. Even my horses would have been on my mind.

But there was no mind with me in heaven, and nothing to ponder...just a knowing that all was well and complete. There were no sensations either. Those belong to the body. They are of this world, not heaven. Nothing of the world makes it to heaven. None of our earthly "equipment" is needed or wanted there. No aid is needed where life is uncontaminated by sin and death.

There is no way I can adequately explain it. No human terms can describe the heavenly things I was allowed to experience.

If only they could.

My awareness in heaven was all about Jesus. I cannot tell you what heaven looks like. I did not see angels; no gates or mansions caught my eye; no heavenly flowers dazzled me. Others have seen these things, but I did not. Some report being reunited with their loved ones. I never saw mine.

Being consumed with His love was more than enough for me. What else could I possibly need? What could I desire that would exceed it? Love is who He is, and it permeates the very atmosphere of heaven. The common denominator of everything He allowed me to experience was love.

I think of what Jesus told the thief who was crucified beside Him on Calvary: "Truly, I tell you, today you will be with me in paradise" (Luke 23:43). My time with Jesus was paradise. As narrowly focused as I was on Him, I was completely satisfied. He was enough for me. There was no curiosity about anything else—no attraction that I feared missing. He revealed what He chose to reveal, and I experienced more than I could have dreamed possible.

In the physical world we try to live in the moment. In heaven the moment is eternity. It is so difficult to describe the timelessness of the place. Yet, that is heaven; it has no beginning or end. There was no looking back or forward in time and no need to fathom time. How "long" I was there was unknown to me. Was it five minutes? Three days? I cannot say. This much I know for certain: the end of the physical, earthly life—what we call death—is not the end at all. It is just the beginning!

Before I arrived in heaven, I thought my ideas about life made sense. Really, nothing I had learned about life was accurate in heaven's terms. It was at best a shadow. I do not mean to diminish the joys of life on Earth. God gives us precious moments that bring great satisfaction. There are moments in our earthly lives when we feel more "alive," as though glimpsing heaven. As wonderful as those moments are, they cannot touch life in heaven. That is something far beyond our ability to grasp.

First Corinthians 13:12 explains why I cannot begin to describe it: "Now we see only a poor reflection as in a mirror; then we shall see face to face. Now I know in part; then I shall know fully, even as I am fully known."

For those who know Jesus as Savior and Lord, you will know as you are known. You will witness the reality of life in heaven! For those who don't yet know Him this way, you can. Just talk with Him. Tell Him that you believe He died on the cross to save you from the stain of sin. Tell Him that you accept the sacrifice He made on your behalf. Then welcome Him into your heart and life as your Savior and Lord.[1] He will make Himself known to you. He will also open heaven's door to you when your time comes to leave this world and enter eternity.

FROM EARTH TO HEAVEN

The Lord did allow me to witness one sight while I was with Him, and it was amazing. I saw prayers rising to heaven—the prayers of those who cried out to God as I lay dead. I did not hear the words they prayed—I saw the prayers themselves.

How I knew they were prayers was the same way I knew anything while I was there—it was communicated Spirit to spirit. There was no ambiguity in heaven about anything, and certainly not about anything Jesus wanted me to know. When He expressed Himself, I knew it was Him, and I knew it was true.

I knew He had chosen to let me see the prayers, and what an experience it was! They shot up to heaven as bolts of light. They made no sound that I could hear, but they were spectacular. First there was one bolt, then another, then a couple more. Looking back, I think the first bolt was the prayer of my friend David Martin, who sat on a fence near where I fell from my horse.

The number of prayers grew rapidly. As suddenly as they started, the handful of bolts became ten and then hundreds. Soon there were thousands of bolts of light shooting upward, each one a single prayer that demanded attention. Jesus did not reveal to me the source of every prayer. I could not tell which of the thousands came from which people. But I saw all of them, and they were awe inspiring.

If I had imagined the most astounding light show on Earth, and then multiplied it exponentially, it would not have matched the wonder of what I saw. Knowing that the bolts were prayers made the heavenly display even more striking. The requests of the saints made their way to heaven! They did not waft up unnoticed. They did not smash into ceilings on Earth and then fall to the ground. They did not evaporate on their way to heaven.

The Bible says, "The prayer of a righteous person is powerful and effective" (James 5:16). I saw how prayers penetrate heaven! The idea of "prayers going up" became more real to me than ever before. They do go up—all the way up! I saw it with my own "eyes."

If I saw the prayers, He did too. More importantly, He heard them.

As my friends and family prayed, I was with the One who would answer them. (What an astounding thought that is!) The light show happened right in front of us. When the number of bolts reached the thousands—how many thousands I cannot say—they exploded into a single mass of light. It was brighter than anything I had ever seen or expected to see. There is no way to describe it or to capture it in words. I can only say that it was very, very bright.

That was when my time in heaven ended. Without warning or opportunity to protest, it was over. He did not ask me whether I wanted to stay with Him or return to Earth. He just sent me back. As quickly as I had departed Earth, I returned.

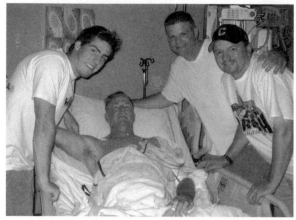

In hospital recovery with my sons Colton Vest, Rowdy Vest, and Denny Webb

At my daughter's high school graduation (from left: Debbie Vest, Colton Vest, Leigh Vest, Rowdy Vest, and myself)

The most blessed day of my life—the day I married Debbie.

My mother and dad and their eighteen children (I'm the little boy my mother is holding at the far right).

Back in the saddle, roping off my horse, Fancy.

It doesn't get any better than this—roping with my friends.

༸ Chapter 6 ༸

BACK in the SADDLE

For to me, to live is Christ and to die is gain. . . . I am torn between the two.
PHILIPPIANS 1:21, 23

E XPLODING LIGHT WAS the last I saw of heaven. The next thing I knew, my spirit and body were reunited, and I was in ICU.

There was no transition or time to adjust. The change overwhelmed me. Gone was the serenity of heaven. My unconfined spirit was now back inside a body strapped to a bed. My aching throat housed a thick breathing tube. Intravenous lines penetrated my hand and neck. Wires went every which way connecting my ailing body to monitors standing sentinel all around me. The seriousness of the situation could not have been clearer.

Immediately I attempted to get up, but a nurse kept me from moving and hurting myself. "Mr. Vest, you're OK," she said calmly.

I thought, "You don't know where I've been. This is not OK. It's not even close to OK."

The nurse was only doing her job, and doing it well. My

return to consciousness had defied the odds. For a professional who knew how unfavorable those odds were, my awakening was akin to a miracle. She could not have known what I was thinking. For me, the negatives were glaring: I obviously could not breathe on my own, so a machine kept me going. I had no idea how long I'd been there, or when—or whether—I would leave.

I thought, "Lord, if this is what I came back for, I want to go back to heaven now."

Dying was easy; it was the easiest thing I'd ever done. The shock of being back—of being alive, at least in earthly terms—that was hard. Living in the confines of my body, with my mind in its usual place, was an awful letdown. Everything in heaven had been so perfect. All forms of pain were behind me; all suffering was done. Or so I thought.

TOUCH AND GO

If I lived long enough, there would be time to figure out why God had sent me back. All I could do now was adjust. It did not take long to appreciate the gift I had received: God had given me another chance to love my beautiful family. I was not sure how much time I had left, but I wanted to make the most of it.

My heart attack stunned them. They were used to various roping accidents, but nothing of this magnitude. I'd suffered heat stroke and gotten banged up doing rodeo. Debbie had received phone calls when I'd been thrown from a horse or met with some other cowboy calamity.

Calf ropers' wives are more or less used to that. Nerve-racking as it is, it's not exactly shocking. But the phone call she and Colton received while at her cousin's house in Mississippi was different. It was the kind of call that changes everything.

Debbie's cousin relayed the message. They were told that I'd been in some sort of accident and was being taken by ambulance to Graham Regional Medical Center. Few details were available, but one thing was clear: it didn't look good. I can only imagine what Debbie and Colton went through being so far away and knowing that I might leave this earth before they could reach me.

Debbie's concern was not about herself, but about me. She could not bear the thought of my being alone, so she called my brother Ocie. Because of where he lived, he could get to Graham faster than anyone else. She explained that I'd been in a bad accident, and Ocie knew what to do.

Debbie also called Rowdy, who is a police officer. Through the phone she heard lots of voices in the background as Rowdy took in the news. He was in the office amid the usual hectic activity. Rowdy is a very polite young man, not given to raising his voice. But at that moment, the police officer's authority rose to the occasion. Debbie listened as he took charge and asked his coworkers to quiet down so he could hear what she was saying.

Debbie then called the hospital and spoke to a nurse who reported that I had been life-flighted to Harris Methodist Hospital in Fort Worth. Paramedics had defibrillated my heart twice on the way to Graham Regional and managed to restore an irregular heartbeat. It was little more than a flutter, really, but it was something. The CareFlite team had to restart my heart twice more in the helicopter.

The nurse took care in clarifying the situation for Debbie, explaining that I had not had an accident but had suffered a massive heart attack. The news remained dismal, but having the correct details was important to Debbie, both as a wife and a nurse. Immediately she passed the new information to Rowdy, who headed to Fort Worth.

Meanwhile in Graham, Nick Burnham began calling my friends and family. Knowing that Debbie and Colton were in Mississippi and Leigh was home alone, Nick called our good friends Todd and Marcy Laughrey. Their daughter, Kaitlyn, had been Leigh's best friend since the fifth grade. The Laughreys were kind enough to go to the house, where Kaitlyn broke the news to Leigh. They explained to Leigh that I had suffered a massive heart attack and I was in really bad shape. They then drove her to Harris.

Both Leigh and Rowdy got there before I was admitted. After doctors looked me over, they asked Rowdy and Leigh some questions about me and about my medical history. Leigh was as straightforward as her mother would have been. She asked the doctor for the bottom line: "Is my daddy going to live?"

His only answer was what Debbie heard in Mississippi: "It doesn't look good."

Debbie and Colton tried to get a commercial flight to Texas, but it was Saturday night and the last flight left at 6:30 p.m. A relative of Debbie's tried to arrange a private flight, but all of his planes were already in the air. Debbie considered driving to Memphis and catching a flight from there, but the logistics were tough and time was slipping away.

With their options running out, the husband of Debbie's cousin offered sound advice. "I'm not telling you what to do," he said, "but if I were you, I'd get in the car and go."

He was right. The road trip would take nine hours, but driving to Memphis, waiting for a departure, flying to Dallas, and driving to Fort Worth could easily take longer. So Debbie, Colton, and a friend of Colton's loaded up the car. Colton and his friend did the driving. Debbie prayed and tried to unwind as much as possible. Mostly she handled a steady stream of calls and updates. It was a long and exhausting ride. She'll pick up the story from here.

In Debbie's Words

It was a long drive to Fort Worth, and it was exhausting. I felt so helpless being so far away from Freddy. I knew the trip would take about nine hours, but it seemed longer, as though the miles would never run out and the wondering would never end.

There was one piece of very good news for which I was thankful: Freddy was in good hands. Harris is an excellent hospital, and they were doing everything possible to stabilize him. They cauterized some heart tissue and were successful in repairing the damage caused by the heart attack. Still, Freddy's long-term prognosis would not be known until later. In those early hours his doctors were more concerned about his immediate survival than anything else.

According to one of the doctors, only 9 percent of people who suffer cardiac arrest survive the event. For each minute without defibrillation, mortality rates spike sharply. Five minutes or maybe ten at the outside are all you have to restore circulation and avoid brain damage.[1]

Colton and I had a lot on our minds during the drive to Fort Worth. Knowing that Rowdy, Leigh, and Ocie were with Freddy eased our minds. We knew that if Freddy was at all aware of his surroundings, their love and support would give him comfort.

Of course, I wished I had been at home when all this happened. Freddy had a number of rodeo accidents while I was gone in the past, but nothing like this. I could hardly believe the circumstances. The odds of my being out of state when my husband needed me most were next to nil. Freddy always tried to ensure that we traveled together. We are rarely separated by distance like we were that weekend.

I knew before I left for Mississippi that Freddy would be roping on Saturday. I also knew that working with horses is dangerous. Life-threatening injuries are always a possibility. Being in rodeo so long, Freddy had his share of close calls. He'd been to the emergency room numerous times for one injury or another. One time he was thrown from his horse and almost broke his neck. Another time his rope snapped back and hit him in the eye. When he put his hand up to his face, he thought for sure he would find his eye resting in it. Thank God, the eye stayed in its socket!

When you marry a cowboy, you accept the fact that accidents come with the territory. As much as I hated to receive emergency calls, I was as prepared for them as a wife can be. Freddy's heart attack was another story, however. It was completely out of the blue, and it was far more serious than anything we had weathered in the past.

I may be a nurse, but my cage was rattled. I was not ready to lose Freddy. I suppose I'll never be ready for that.

WAKE-UP CALL

We arrived at the hospital at 3:30 a.m. on Sunday. The dimly lit waiting room was filled with family and friends. Some had pillows and blankets and were napping in chairs. Others talked quietly amongst themselves. It was so good to see the family!

Freddy's sister Trenna led Colton and me straight to Freddy's room, where Rowdy and Leigh were already keeping vigil. Even as a nurse I was not sure what to expect. I knew that Freddy was very seriously ill. Nine hours of communication with doctors made that crystal clear. They and Freddy's nurses never hid the gravity of the situation from me. It may be that they were more direct than usual, knowing I was a nurse.

In any case, I was well informed. Still, nothing could have prepared me for the moment I walked into Freddy's room. Seeing him hit me hard. He looked helpless and almost lifeless. The sight of my husband on a respirator, with tubes coming and going from all over his body, was overwhelming. "This is not good," I thought. "This is not good at all."

Doctors soon confirmed my assessment. One doctor explained all the measures they had taken to save Freddy's life. They had used virtually everything in their bag of tricks. "Now it is in God's hands," he said solemnly. "If your husband does survive, there's a good chance he will live out his life in a vegetative state."

The doctor's frankness and my experience in the medical field brought home the enormity of the situation. I wondered what I could do and realized it was what I had done all along—pray, pray, pray. Freddy had made it this far; I would pray for his complete recovery. At least now I was there beside him to support and encourage him, to whatever degree I was able to reach him.

Reaching him would not be easy. Because of the breathing tube, Freddy was heavily sedated. Rowdy kept talking to his dad, regardless of his level of consciousness. When he announced to Freddy that Colton and I were there, Freddy began to move. He was responding! He was still in restraints, so all he could manage was to raise his hands to his stomach, but it was a big moment—a huge moment.

Rowdy did his father and me proud. I was so touched by the way he stepped up to the plate. In his usual humble way, he credited his sister with being the strong one. She was strong. All of our children were strong. Still, Rowdy texted me while Colton and I were still on the road; he wrote: "Leigh is holding it together for us. I'm not so strong, but she is."

That's Rowdy...sweet, strong, humble Rowdy. Long before the ordeal was over, we saw the amazing strength and grace of Leigh and Colton too.

Before Colton and I arrived, Freddy tried to communicate with Rowdy and Leigh via hand gestures. He made a move as if he were roping. Rowdy realized what he was trying to say and said, "Don't worry, Dad. Your horses are OK. Mike and Wesley got them back to the barn." Cowboy that Freddy is, horses were on his mind.

Once Colton and I were there, Freddy tried to communicate again. He explained later that although he could not see us, he heard our voices. He knew exactly who was in the room and where each one was in relation to his bed. Soon he started pointing back and forth. His range of motion was very limited by the restraints, but his actions were deliberate. It was encouraging to see him acting so decisively.

Unfortunately we had no idea what Freddy was trying to say. I am sure I looked like a deer in the headlights. I was at a complete loss to understand the meaning behind the movements. Rowdy saw the look on my face and set out to decipher his dad's hand language. Rowdy would not quit until we understood the message Freddy was working so hard to get across. "Dad," said Rowdy, "if it takes all night, we'll figure out what you're saying."

Freddy continued. He pointed at Leigh, then at himself, then at his heart, and finally at Leigh again. He did the same with Colton, Rowdy, and me. Finally, we got it— he was telling each of us that he loved us. What a precious moment it was! None of us will ever forget it.

Freddy told me later that he did not know whether he would make it through to morning or how long he would be around. He did not want to leave this earth a second time without telling us how much he loved us.

It was a lot like what Freddy's father had done on his deathbed years before. Lee Roy Vest said good-bye with his eyes and made sure everyone knew that he loved them. The apple doesn't fall far from the tree. Freddy loves his family too and puts them ahead of himself. Even with his life hanging in the balance, he wanted to minister to us.

Freddy made the most of those moments. He probably did not know what his doctors were thinking: they were amazed that he was still alive. "There is no medical reason that he is still with us," one doctor said. "The only possible explanation is that God was not ready for Freddy at this time."

Freddy's chances of seeing the sunrise were less than 5 percent. The doctor told us, "If there's anything you need to say to him, you should take this opportunity to say it."

Somehow Freddy had gotten the memo.

When I first met Freddy back in the day, his mom

was hospitalized in intensive care. He so wanted me to meet her that he got me into ICU. With a family as big as his, hospital staff were willing to believe that just about anyone in Texas was kin.

How sweet it was to meet Mama and the rest of Freddy's family! The waiting room was teeming with relatives. Everyone was so open and warm. They didn't know me, but they hugged me as if they did and made me feel like one of the family.

From the beginning I felt comfortable with the Vest clan. It was so easy to fit in and be myself around them. There was no need to impress anyone. No one put on airs with me either. For an only child who dreamed of being part of a family like Freddy's, I could not imagine one more kind and generous than they were. It was easy to see why he was that way too.

Now more than twenty years later, the family rallied around Freddy and gave Rowdy, Colton, Leigh, and me tremendous comfort. It absolutely meant the world to us.

Grace for the Pressure

Freddy's heart attack was the kind of event that makes you think, "I cannot handle all of this." There were so many "what ifs." I had worked through most of them during the drive from Mississippi. "What if he doesn't make it? What if there's brain damage? How extensive would it be?" The list seemed endless. I wished I could just postpone the questions and hope for the best, but I knew I had to deal with them and move forward.

By God's grace I did. Once at the hospital I shifted into a different gear. It was not about "what ifs," but about being in the moment and continuing in prayer. I would get away by myself to pray whenever possible. People's prayers brought Freddy back; prayers now would help us navigate the road ahead. There were many tough decisions to make. I could not afford to live in the past or the future. There was a cause to fight for, and it was now.

That cause was Freddy's life. Doctors said it was touch and go with Freddy. Medically speaking, they were absolutely right. Yet I knew we had to fight through the bad news and focus on the good. Freddy was communicating. He was far from 100 percent, but he was aware and making an effort to stay connected with us. As far as my kids and I were concerned, he had a chance to make it, and we were going to support that chance any way we could.

Freddy's heart attack happened on Saturday. On Sunday he started waking up more often, but he was still on the respirator. I was eager for doctors to take him off the machine, because the longer respiratory assistance is used, the harder it is for the patient to do without it. Also, the sedatives masked Freddy's neurological condition. Doctors would not be able to assess his brain function until the drugs wore off.

The doctors understood my concerns but would not take Freddy off the respirator until his own breathing capacity reached a certain percentage level. He stayed on the machine through Sunday, therefore, he also remained sedated. Patients have to be heavily sedated to tolerate a large tube down the throat. Unless they are drugged, they would be tempted to yank it out.

On Monday doctors began the process of weaning Freddy from the ventilator. They turned the machine off, but left the tube in, just in case. If he continued to breathe on his own for an hour, they would remove the tube.

Sure enough he continued to breathe—unassisted! What an answer to prayer it was! Because of his medication Freddy did not seem to notice at first that the tube was gone. But as the sedation wore off, he came alive and wasted no time getting back in the flow. He talked with visitors, thanked them, and held their hands. It was so good to see him being Freddy again.

During these visits Freddy often became very emotional. We worried about the interaction being too draining. Meanwhile he was concerned about how his emotions were affecting everyone else. That's Freddy for you!

The ICU team had done all they could to accommodate such a large family. Knowing that Freddy's chances of making it were low, they were lenient with visitor restrictions. They were very sensitive and kind in bending the rules, but because the interaction was so exhausting to Freddy, we limited visitation anyway, hoping it would help him regain strength.

Freddy is a very tenderhearted man, yet he is not normally prone to having uncontrollable emotions. During the early hours of his recovery he would easily come to tears and be unable to stop crying. Some visits affected him more than others. An excellent nurse helped him and us to understand that a lack of emotional control after a heart attack is perfectly normal. A little medication helped even things out, and Freddy came through that sensitive period with flying colors.

Seeing Freddy respond to loved ones was so encouraging to us and to his medical team. He regained his bearings quickly and did a great job of linking faces with names. Certain details escaped his memory, but that was to be expected.

We were excited when Freddy said he wanted to get cleaned up. It was a good sign of his progress. Patients who are detached from their surroundings care little about grooming, so his wishes gave us hope. Freddy was fighting the good fight!

Without realizing it, he gave us another encouraging sign during a conversation with his doctor. The doctor asked, "Mr. Vest, what is the last thing you remember before your heart attack?"

In a flash Freddy cracked a joke. "Doc, I don't remember the last time I broke wind, much less anything about a heart attack."

It was not a Southern gal's idea of how to speak to a physician. In fact, I was mortified, my face beet red. The doctor was not the least bit embarrassed. He just kept looking intently at Freddy. Then he turned to me and said, "That's a very good sign. Humor is a higher level of thinking."

Whew! My face returned to its normal shade. Freddy's quip answered our questions about brain damage. Over my embarrassment, I embraced the moment. I enjoy thinking about it even now. Humor is a big part of who

Freddy is. His goofy joke showed me that he was back in the saddle!

Freddy has always been a wonderful man and an amazing husband. Since his heart attack he is even more loving than before. His experience in heaven filled him with God's love and gave him a deeper understanding of God's heart. I doubt he or anyone could have learned the things he did without going to heaven—and coming back.

I try to imagine seeing prayers going up to heaven the way Freddy did. It had such an effect on him. How could it not? Having a second chance with his family affected him too. Things that used to seem important to Freddy aren't important anymore. He is calmer and gentler than ever, and he is more focused on people than he was before (and he was always focused on others).

What happened to Freddy has affected the whole family and most everyone who knows him. We are so thankful to have another chance to love him. Things that used to distract us don't get in the way anymore. When something goes haywire in life, we get over it quickly. We are more focused on enjoying our time together than on everything being perfect. We truly are more closely knit than ever. Even our kids want to hang around us more. They like staying close to us, even though they are adults with lives of their own. Freddy and I are loving it!

There is no doubt in my mind that God sent Freddy back with a mission. He has great compassion for those who are sick or dying and for those who have lost loved ones prematurely. He is able to comfort them and their loved ones in ways few people can. Going to heaven has given him something special to share with others. It reminds me of a passage of Scripture:

> Praise be to the God and Father of our Lord Jesus Christ, the Father of compassion and the God of all comfort, who comforts us in all our troubles, so that we can comfort those in any trouble with the comfort we ourselves receive from God.
> —2 CORINTHIANS 1:3–4

Freddy's new assignment is a wonderful part of his testimony—a part he will share in coming chapters. First, he'll tell you more about his return from heaven. It is quite a story!

TAKING CARE OF "BUSINESS"

Being hooked up to a ventilator makes your priorities very clear. I did not know what got me there; I only knew that I was enjoying heaven while my family was going through the mill.

Whether or not I would leave the hospital alive was uncertain. Going back to heaven seemed like a really good option to me. It was also a very likely one. Yet I knew it would be hard on Debbie and the kids. There was not much I could do about that except to give them some closure. I could not leave without saying good-bye and letting them know how deeply I loved them.

So I did both. Hand motions were all I could muster at the time. They were limited motions at that, but they would have to do. It was like playing charades but with my hands tied down. Nobody knew what I was trying to say; they promised they would not quit till they figured it out.

Finally someone caught on and asked, "Are you saying that you love Leigh?"

I nodded and thought, "Thank God! They got it!" I was going to tell my kids Daddy loved them if it was the last thing I did. The same goes for Debbie. I had to express my love to her. It's not as though she and the kids didn't know I loved them, but saying it might be the last thing I could give them. At that point nothing else mattered. It was quite possibly the reason God sent me back.

There was one other thing I needed to say. It would take more than hand motions to get it across, so it would have to wait until the vent was removed from my throat.

Even after I came off the ventilator, I knew I was not out of the woods, so I asked Debbie and Rowdy to come in—nobody else, just the two of them.

I got right to the point and told Rowdy how much I loved Debbie. "If I don't make it," I said, "I want you to be sure Colton and Leigh understand how I feel. Debbie is only forty-eight years old, too young to go through the rest of her life alone. She has too much love in her heart to live that way. When the time is right, she needs to remarry."

If Debbie had known ahead of time what I was going to say, she would have stopped me. I knew she would not want me to talk this way, and I knew she did not want to think about life after my demise. But the subject was important, and I said my piece.

"Rowdy, I need you to help the kids understand that this is my wish for Debbie. I don't want her to be alone. It's OK with me for her to settle down with another man after I'm gone."

Rowdy promised to honor my wishes. I was proud to entrust my son with the responsibility; I knew he would keep his word. It was important for Debbie to know how I felt, but it was also important for the rest of the family to be in agreement. That way there would be no guilt or hesitation, and Debbie could find happiness again, knowing that she had everyone's blessing.

Debbie and I have always believed that we would leave this world together. Now it looked as if things could unfold differently. She needed to hear from my lips to her ears that I loved her enough to desire her happiness, even if it wasn't shared with me. There was no need for her to wonder how any of us would feel if she found a good man who treated her right. I wanted her life to be wonderful for as many years as God gave her.

For me, the situation was win-win: If I stayed, I had the most amazing wife and children to come home to. If I didn't make it, I would return to the place that had won my heart for all eternity. "For to me, to live is Christ and to die is gain" (Phil. 1:21).

A Place Beyond Words

Visiting heaven was a life-altering experience—so intense that I dared not speak of it lightly. Not even my family would know the story until a couple days after I came back. Even then I could share only some of my feelings. The experience was so personal and difficult to articulate! Where would I begin?

Ever since I died it has been of the utmost importance to me that I share only what the Lord wants me to share, when He wants me to share it. After my hospital stay I tried to be sensitive to Debbie and the kids, not gloating about heaven, but sharing the experience that changed my life. I sat on my back porch for three months doing little more than smiling all the time. I was so blessed to be with my family again. My love for them had only grown deeper, and I relished every moment with them.

I still do. Yet as precious as they are to me, I would not have come back if I had been given the option to stay in heaven with the Lord. The choice would have been a no-brainer. I know for sure that I would not have left heaven of my own accord.

If you are married, and especially if you have children, that might sound coldhearted. It is not like coming back to my family would have "invalidated" my "ticket" to heaven. Not at all. I would never lose out on eternity with Him simply by returning to my earthly life.

So how can I explain my desire to stay in heaven? The truth is that I cannot. Heaven and Earth are entirely different realms. Trying to explain the effect of heaven on a believer is like trying to articulate what you feel when you become a parent, only harder.

Heaven is not the way most of us think it is. If you go there, you will know what I mean. The attraction to the place is not a mental thing; my brain did not go with me to heaven. Whether I wanted to stay or go was not a matter of "making up my mind." It was a purely spiritual bond—a sense of being in the place where I belonged with the One who created me. I was home. Everything of the world dissolves in heaven. When you are there, nothing else matters but Jesus.

Often I think about the Scripture passage in which some religious folks asked Jesus about the afterlife. Their questions reveal how earthbound our human thinking is:

> "Teacher," they said, "Moses told us that if a man dies without having children, his brother must marry the widow and raise up offspring for him. Now there were seven brothers among us. The first one married and died, and since he had no children, he left his wife to his brother. The same thing happened to the second and third brother, right on down to the seventh. Finally, the woman died. Now then, at the resurrection, whose wife will she be of the seven, since all of them were married to her?"
>
> Jesus replied, "You are in error because you do not know the Scriptures or the power of God. At the resurrection people will neither marry nor be given in marriage."
>
> —MATTHEW 22:24–30

They were thinking in human terms about a place that operates on God's terms. They were concerned about rules and regulations and about who belonged to whom. Jesus tried to help them see that heaven does not conform to our natural understanding of how things work. In essence He said, "You don't understand, because you cannot understand yet. But trust Me; it's not like you think."

Talking about heaven in human language is next to impossible to do. I can do it only with His leading; even then I'm at a loss to tell it exactly as it is. I know I am not the only one who struggles to explain it. When I speak to individuals or groups, I can almost always tell which ones have been to heaven and back. The looks on their faces say it all. If I'm speaking publicly, they will pull me aside afterward and say, "It's exactly like you said it is. I've never told anybody about it. I just can't. I wouldn't know where to begin."

Having met or been in touch with a good number of people who have been to heaven, I can tell you what they never say. The never say: "Yes! The same thing happened to me, and I couldn't wait to tell everybody."

Of course, I cannot speak for anyone but myself. I do know this much: being in heaven with Jesus is an intensely private experience—so private it almost seems off limits for conversation. When people hear my testimony, it seems to break the ice. Those who have been to heaven seem more comfortable after hearing my story. They trickle up to me and say, "Hey, I've been there. I know what you're talking about!"

I'm often the first person they have ever told. It may be that hearing it from me helps them to know that their experiences were real. I can tell you for sure that when they open up and share their testimonies with me, it gives me comfort too. It confirms that I'm doing a God thing by reaching out to them.

▶•◀▶•◀▶•◀

By the grace of God I have received two gifts I cannot possibly deserve. The first was the experience of being with my Lord in heaven. It has made me a different man, one who will never be done saying, "Thank You, Lord." The second is also powerful: the privilege of a brand-new season with my family. It is a richer time than I could have imagined, and I have embraced it with every cell of my being.

Today, my loved ones know where I was when my heart stopped beating. They have heard the details I just shared with you. But they did not learn everything at once. It took a couple days for me to open up even a little bit. It took longer than that to tell them the whole story.

Sharing it with them has been one of the great joys of my life.

✐Chapter 7✐

The WHY and the WHERE

Here is the test to find whether your mission on Earth is finished: if you're alive, it isn't.[1]
Richard Bach

A PART FROM THE prayers I saw, I never got to see the beauty of heaven. But God allowed me to experience it. That was enough to overflow this cowboy's cup!

Now I can tell you without a shred of doubt: heaven is real, and so is Jesus. If He is your Savior and Lord, you have nothing to fear about death—nothing. Notice that I said, "If Jesus is your Savior and Lord." If He is not, then there is plenty to fear about death. Heaven is real, but so is hell.

Hell was not meant to be your eternal home. There is no reason for you to go there! Jesus paid the price for you to be saved. I mentioned this in chapter 5, but it bears repeating: a simple prayer will change your eternal destiny. You can pray the following or use words of your own:

Jesus, I repent of my sins and I receive You as my Savior and Lord. I believe that You died for my sake, to cleanse me of all sin. Thank You for Your precious sacrifice and for making me a new creation. Amen.

The invitation to heaven is addressed to your loved ones too. If your loved one is nearing the end of this physical life and knows Jesus as Savior and Lord, you can have perfect peace knowing that he or she will spend eternity with Him. I know how hard it is to lose the ones we love, but I can promise you there is no more wonderful destination than heaven. Your loved one will never suffer or be sorrowful there. He or she will never want to leave and will only look forward to the day that you will know the glories of the place!

I have no doubt that when I die again Jesus will keep me in heaven. I look forward to that day, but I'm no longer looking for the eject button out of this life. Being with my family gets better and better. Not only that, but I have also discovered why I am here. Knowing that changes everything.

Reentry and a New Me

Those first hours of consciousness in the ICU were too intense for figuring out what happened and what was to come. There were so many hoops to jump through first, whether spiritually, emotionally, or physically. There was a lengthy recuperation period ahead. It would give me plenty of time to figure everything out.

Having been in the bosom of Jesus, I knew He would help me. After all, He was the One who sent me back to this life. He also gave me the perfect place to regroup: our back porch. For months I sat there, looking at the lake and reflecting. My incessant smiling made everyone curious. When Debbie and the kids asked what I was thinking about, the only answer I could give them was to smile some more.

Our family had been on one crazy roller coaster ride. My experience was very different from theirs, however. I went to heaven. My visit was short but incredibly sweet. They were in this world facing the loss of a husband and father. Although I pulled through, it was hard for them to talk about my dying. Even the best parts of my story reminded them of what had almost happened. It is still difficult for them to think about going on without me.

Talking about your own death is a rare experience. Those who come back from it see death differently from most other people. A friend and I were talking some time ago. He made a great point about how going to heaven changes things. "Freddy," he said, "what can anybody threaten you with? Death?"

He is exactly right. The idea of dying is not scary to me—not anymore. I'm not in a rush to check out because I know God sent me back. Even though it was not my choice, I trust Him in it. Either way I can promise you that, for me, the threat of death would fall on deaf ears.

That is what I call blessed assurance! Death truly has

no sting (see 1 Corinthians 15:55). At the same time, life means much more than it did before my death. My awareness of life is heightened, sometimes to the point of extremes. This was especially noticeable during my recuperation. Things that never got my attention suddenly jumped out at me with new meaning and intensity.

One morning I noticed a honeybee that had fallen into our swimming pool. This was not the kind of thing I noticed before I went to heaven. Now I was not only aware of the bee but also felt compelled to rescue the poor thing. I got a skimmer net, fished him out, and let him dry off. Helping the bee mattered to me. I wanted him to live and fly again. I saw in his drenched body the preciousness of life, and I was reminded of the millions of people who need to be rescued, dried off, and made free.

After being in heaven, I could not return to business as usual. As they say, "There's no way to get there from here." The Freddy who died and went to heaven was not the same Freddy who returned to Earth. I could not just pick up where I left off; I needed to understand the reason for my journey. The "new Freddy" needed to know exactly where the "dead Freddy" had been and why he was sent back to be reunited with his body.

These questions preoccupied me for months. Nobody could fill in the blanks for me; I needed answers from God. Without them I would miss the point of the extreme events my family and I had been through. All I wanted was to make the most of the time I was given. I wanted to understand His plan so I could do what He asked of me. Without His answers I would be a changed man walking in the dark.

GOD SETTLES THE WHY

In the months after my heart attack friends were kind to come and visit. What beautiful times of fellowship we had! It was poignant just to see them again.

Some friends asked about my death and about where I went when my heart stopped beating. Debbie was the first to share the details. At some point I began sharing too. With certain people, I knew I was supposed bring up the subject. Even so, I didn't know how they would take what I had to say. They might have scratched their heads and thought I was some kind of nut. But I had no choice; I had to risk it. God was telling me to speak, and I was committed to obeying Him.

There was another side to that coin. Sometimes I spoke without knowing it was God's idea. It was not a showboating thing. Sharing my testimony was more of a challenge than a lark. It stirred up lots of emotions and took everyone out of their comfort zones. Yet I knew He sent me back for a purpose. I felt pressed to make good use of the time He had given me. The pressure was not from Him but from me. My intentions were good, but I was trying too hard to make something happen for the Lord—as though He needed my help.

When I acted on my own, it always ended in a blunder. I remember trying to talk to a cowboy friend of mine. I say trying because it was a struggle. The words would not come, and whatever words I did manage to eke out seemed to boomerang without accomplishing anything but confusion. The poor guy could not make heads or tails of what I was saying. Neither could I! I remember telling myself, "I need to quit this."

After banging my head against the wall more times than I can count, I realized that God would have to tell me when to speak and when to shut up. For months I prayed each morning that He would do so. As I prayed this way, the larger questions about why I am here and what I am supposed to be doing got answered.

Thank God! I was desperate for His guidance. What happened in heaven was too precious to just blab here, there, and everywhere. At the same time I knew that hearing about my experience would comfort others who either feared death or were curious about heaven and eternity. I did not want to withhold my testimony just because I was afraid of making a mistake. What I wanted more than anything was for hurting hearts to be healed.

You can trust that if you ask God for guidance He will oblige and settle the issue. And did He ever settle mine! He did not give me a complicated revelation or a ten-point checklist. He answered me the way He knows I learn best: He wrote down the answer. Actually He had put it in black and white centuries before the day it reached me. His timing was perfect, and His message was clear:

> You must go to everyone I send you to and say
> whatever I command you.
> —JEREMIAH 1:7

God changed my life with fifteen words! Instantly I knew that He really had dispatched me from heaven for a reason. He knew I was a simple man, and He tailored His message in the simplest way. He would send me to specific people, and He would tell me what to say! That was something this calf roper could say yes to!

From that point on there was no experimenting to get it right. God spared other cowboys (and everyone else) from my garbled messages that did more harm than good. Now I am content to leave it all up to God. If it's His idea, I don't have to worry about messing up. As long as I speak to the ones He sends me, and as long as I share what He gives me, they will be touched by Him. Even when He gives me no words at all, I don't worry a lick. Sometimes a smile is a seed that someone else can water.

The freedom from those fifteen words is priceless. It's like what Jesus said: "The Son can do nothing by himself; he can do only what he sees his Father doing, because whatever the Father does the Son also does" (John 5:19). I'm not doing "my thing"; this is His doing. What He wants to accomplish in people's hearts is not my business. I don't need to figure it out. All I need to do is obey Him. He knows what the needs are, and He knows how to address them.

Nor is it my job to make sure people receive what He sends me to say. For example, when I speak before groups, I am OK with knowing that not everyone believes my testimony. Their believing is between them and God. There is no pressure for me to make sure they heard me right. My job is to put it out there; He works with it as He sees fit.

The mission is His. The timing is His. Even the words are His. Knowing that makes it easy, whatever the calling.

THE TRUTH MADE ME FREE

All my life I did what fathers and mothers do for their families—I worked hard to provide for them. I have been blessed with interesting lines of work. Like my daddy, I like to work, and I'm thankful for God's provision for my family.

Before I died, I was like a lot of people, maybe even most people—I felt it was my job to make things happen in business. When the Lord called me to work for Him, I applied the same formula. It was the only one I knew.

I am glad it took only a number of months and not another five decades to figure that one out! The moment God said, "You must go to everyone I send you to and say whatever I command you" (Jer. 1:7), I understood what to do and how to do it. His Word gave me complete peace. I did not hesitate to speak when He asked me to, and I was comfortable saying nothing when He asked me to be still.

Another time He spoke to me in stronger terms. No doubt, I needed it. "This is My business," He said. "All you have to do is do what I say and tell you to do. Other than that, go and enjoy roping."

God certainly has a sense of humor, and He knows how to talk to cowboys too!

I cannot tell you how He freed me up. Knowing that it is His business took a load off my shoulders. It also made me stronger and more settled in who I am. There is no worrying or wavering because I know He is taking care of everything—and doing a far better job of it than I ever could.

Life was much more difficult before He taught me these things. All my life I had tried to carry burdens that were not mine to carry. I was so busy doing His part that I could not get my part straight. Now, at the end of the day, I lay my head on the pillow in peace. I simply pray, "Lord, I did my best to obey You. I pray You'll count me worthy."

You cannot miss when you do your rightful part and not His. That is all He asks, and at the end of it He can say, "Well done, good and faithful servant!...Come and share your master's happiness!" (Matt. 25:23).

Whether it's roping, business, or ministry, He is in charge and He has the answers. He knows what is best and when to do it. All my life is His business. He has orchestrated every event to get me here. He is still orchestrating and confirming His presence and power continually. I do not need to question Him on anything. Even when it seems a stretch for me to believe He will do what He said, I know He is the God who does amazing and inexplicable things!

If He can bring back a guy from the dead, He can do anything. I know that better than I did before. It finally got past my head and into my heart. Whatever the issue in life, I can turn to Him with confidence, knowing what He will say: "Don't worry, Freddy. I got this."

That is music to this man's ears.

NOW FOR THE WHERE

God's calling and instruction answered one of the two big questions I had—the why question. The other question was where. When I died, where exactly did I go?

The wondering started after I came home from the hospital and had some time to reflect. I never questioned whether I was in His presence. I knew I had been with Him in the place He was. There was no distance or separation between us. We were one on one—the most intense communion I have ever experienced or could have imagined.

The where question lingered because I never saw where I was. The prayers that shot up to heaven were the only things I saw. Other than what I'd read in Scripture, I had no idea what the place looked like. I had no frame of reference besides the fact that I was with Him. Had all this happened in my mind? Or were Jesus and I hanging out somewhere in space? The questions baffled me.

God understood my questions and was faithful to answer them. Once again, He wrote them down—in Scripture! It was a sweet process of revelation. I had never before searched the Bible about heaven's location.

I knew three heavens were mentioned, but what distinguished them I did not know. Day by day He showed me.

The process began with the facts. For one thing, there was no doubt that I had died. The EMTs documented that fact. Not that I ever wondered about it. I knew I'd left behind my body and everything that went with it, including my mind. I knew that I was no longer in the world but with Jesus, where He is. My body was on the rodeo grounds, but I was somewhere else—meaning my spirit was somewhere else.

God so graciously answered the where through the testimony of the apostle Paul. It turns out he wrote about the same experience I had in his letter to the church at Corinth. His experience was very real, but even he could not describe it. What little he did say gave me important clues:

> I know a man in Christ who fourteen years ago was caught up to the third heaven. Whether it was in the body or out of the body I do not know—God knows. And I know that this man— whether in the body or apart from the body I do not know, but God knows—was caught up to paradise and heard inexpressible things, things that no one is not permitted to tell.
>
> —2 CORINTHIANS 12:2–4

Bingo! My question was answered, and the place I visited was mentioned in God's Book. All the wondering about not seeing the place and not having words to describe it was resolved. Man simply cannot express the presence of the Lord as he experiences it in heaven. Although Paul concluded that he was caught up to the third heaven and called it by name, even he was at a loss to describe it. Still, his words resonated in my heart; I knew this was the place I visited!

Paul's experience matches mine. I too "heard" things in heaven. But the communication Jesus and I shared did not use words as we know them on Earth. Paul said he heard inexpressible things that a man cannot utter. Only in heaven can you communicate perfectly from spirit to Spirit! Only in heaven can you hear what is inexpressible.

There is more to the three heavens; I will share the rest of what He has given me to share in coming pages. The point here is that the mystery of my whereabouts was solved. I was in the third heaven, which is paradise, the unfathomable place where the spirit man goes into the presence of God.

God solved another part of the mystery for me: I was in heaven, but it was not the eternal heaven. That is the place we tend to speak of and envision as heaven. I never saw that place because I did not go there.

When my body lay in the rodeo dust, as people prayed and as Eddy and Don worked so hard to revive me, I was in the third heaven. It is amazing to think that I have been to a place described in Holy Writ. What peace it gave me to know that the great apostle who wrote two-thirds of the New Testament—Paul himself—could not put the place into any better words than this Texas cowboy could!

Sent to Others

Never did I see myself as one God would use in a public way. I was happy living my life in private, doing the things I love to do—enjoying my family and building homes. Of course, I still love calf roping, which seems more public than my other passions. Even so, what happens in roping is mostly between you, your horse, the clock, and the calf that fights you tooth and nail.

When the Lord gave me His plan from Jeremiah 1:7, He changed my agenda in a big way. He asked me to step out in a more public arena and discuss the most personal experience a person can have—with people I don't know. I never expected that.

As big and unexpected a change as it is, I have given myself to His plan, and my decision is not up for reconsideration. There is no way I could keep the message He has given me to myself. I could not do it if I tried! I understand what the prophet Jeremiah experienced:

> But if I say, "I will not mention his word or speak any more in his name," his word is in my heart like a fire, a fire shut up in my bones. I am weary of holding it in; indeed, I cannot.
>
> —Jeremiah 20:9

How can I hold back what God has given me so freely? How can I hoard it, knowing the comfort it brings?

I cannot.

If you think about it (and Scripture bears it out), all fear boils down to the same root: the fear of death.

When it is answered with God's ultimate peace—when you know that death has been settled through the death and resurrection of Jesus Christ—nothing can make you afraid.

I had been taught that, and I knew it. Yet until I went to heaven, I knew it intellectually. Now I know it experientially. Jesus did solve the issue of death, and He solved it completely. My going to heaven attests to that! It is the reason I could be at such peace with Him. There was nothing left to be done or fixed or corrected. It was finished!

Those who call Him Savior can rest in peace for real and forever. That is why the Christian need not fear anything, not even death. The writer of Hebrews explains it perfectly:

> Since the children have flesh and blood, he too shared in their humanity so that by his death he might break the power of him who holds the power of death—that is, the devil—and free those who all their lives were held in slavery by their fear of death.
> —HEBREWS 2:14–15

That is one giant gulp of hope! I have seen that hope release people from terrible burdens of fear. For some it is the fear of their own deaths. For others it is the anguish of watching a loved one die from disease. Still others are pained by the shock of a loved one's sudden death or the death of a child. For many if not most of these people, death and pain cannot be separated, and grief seems unending. The fear of death holds them in bondage. In other words, they are suffering the torment of fear.

This is true even in the church. Many Christians dread death. Some mourn their loved ones so bitterly that they remain incapacitated or disconnected for years to come. My heart breaks for these people; I know the Lord longs to set them free from death's control.

Why He would choose me to minister to them, I cannot say. But I know that God is not haphazard or random. For whatever reason He allowed this cowboy to experience death, heaven, and a resurrection. I'm no preacher, but as long as He is opening the doors, I will say yes and walk on through.

When God is involved, there is no telling where an open door might lead. I am able to speak to all kinds of people, from professors to cowboys. Because of my background and the relationships I have in the rodeo, I talk with cowboys a lot, whether in cowboy church or between rounds of roping. Like anyone else, they are more likely to listen to someone with whom they can identify. Whether or not they believe me is another story, but they are willing to hear me out, if only because I'm a cowboy.

Roping is still a passion for me, but it's even better now because I have something of eternal value to share with my rodeo friends. Cowboys are a rugged bunch; they live with risk and never quit. Not much scares them, but they hurt like anyone else. When they hear about what God did in my life, they light up. I count it an honor to share my story with them.

At my very first meeting at a small cowboy church, a man in his forties sat in the second row and was very affected by what I shared. Afterward he approached me; he had the telltale look of someone who has been to heaven. Sure enough, he explained that he drowned at the age of twelve. Like me, he was gone awhile. He said, "I've never told anyone all these years. I often wanted to tell my parents, but I didn't even tell them."

I wondered whether he would ever tell them, until he said, "They're both gone now."

I have had so many conversations like this one, in so many settings. Once a woman in an assisted living facility heard my testimony and gave me a big grin afterward. Her eyes sparkled as she confided, "It's exactly like you said. I've been there!"

People who have been to heaven tend to stand out. They have a certain peace, and like the woman in assisted living, they are OK with the thought of death. They don't run from it or run to it. They are ready for it and not the least bit worried about leaving Planet Earth.

God sends me to these people, and often He sends them to me. They are not the only unique group, however. I also speak to those who are terminally ill. Like anyone coming to grips with imminent death and facing the unknown, they worry about what is ahead. Once they hear about heaven, they see death in a new way. Instead of being terrified, they are excited! They look forward to a place far better than any they have ever known.

They make comments such as, "I'm OK now. I'm good with what's ahead."

Once a lady with terminal cancer found peace when I shared my testimony in Sunday school. If you or a loved one has ever had cancer, you know that cancer patients have a lot on their plates. Many suffer in extreme pain. Treatment can be debilitating. Weight loss and other physical changes add to the stress. When a doctor says you are terminal...well, it doesn't get much tougher than that. To see a terminal patient freed from the fear of death is a blessing too big to describe!

Fears of death and dying affect loved ones too. It is especially painful when a child dies or a family member is cut down in his or her prime. Survivors are often tormented by the thought of a loved one's life being cut short. They often say, "He was taken too early," or, "She was cheated out of her best years."

Their grief is heartrending. No one who hasn't been in their shoes can understand their pain. Yet for those who have been to heaven, there is another side of the story that cannot be overlooked. In earthly terms the cutting short of physical life is a devastating loss. But in eternal terms real life starts when the physical body perishes. When a person dies at a young age, he or she is granted this real life—this perfectly amazing life—sooner than expected!

The one who goes to heaven is not suffering but enjoying the bliss we all crave. Those of us who are left behind do the suffering. It is as I said: Dying is easy. Living is hard.

My mother knew this before she left us. I remember visiting her at a nursing home after she had a stroke. None of us wanted her to leave this earth, but she had other ideas. Mama said, "I don't know why God hasn't taken me home yet. I'm ready to go."

She was ready. Shortly after that conversation, Mama went on to her reward. I know beyond a shadow of a doubt that she has never regretted leaving.

PRESSING FORWARD

Like Mama, I never regretted leaving either. Nor did I comprehend (at least at first) why God cut short my stay in heaven. Learning why God sent me back here made all the difference. I can deal with not being in heaven but only because I know what my purpose is on earth.

That is not the statement of a religious man. I have been to heaven, but I don't claim to have my spiritual ducks all in row. There are times when my intentions are good but my desire and willingness to do God's will fall short.

I am a Christian. I am called. I am also human. There are days when I would rather be doing something other than what He has in mind. To pretend that I am spiritually ablaze every moment of my life would be just that—a pretense. At times I'd rather stick to my roping. I'd like to show up at the rodeo, do my thing, and move on.

God knows me well enough to know when I'm in that place. He doesn't throw in the towel and regret the day He called me. He already made the calling easy by removing the guesswork and the guilt; He knows about the day-to-day challenges humans face. Jesus said, "The spirit is willing, but the flesh is weak" (Matt. 26:41). So God graciously works with me; He gives me the grace I need as I need it.

Going back to Jeremiah 1:7 helps me regroup. It reminds me that this is His business and His agenda. None of it is too heavy because He made it light. I don't have to run from pillar to post trying to get everyone saved. That is what I thought at first, and it did not work. Thank God He freed me of that misconception early on.

You might remember something I tell my friends about heaven: "There are no 'gotta dos' there." In heaven every pressure dissolves and every tendency to make something happen stays behind with your corpse.

I'm more able to live without "gotta dos" than I was before I died. Even when my focus slips, I can rest in His care, His agenda, His priorities, His grace, and His strength. He takes care of everything else. He schedules me to speak where He wants me to speak. Without any solicitation from me, churches and other groups invite me. I never set up a website. I do no advertising or name-dropping. It is all Him, and that is exactly how it needs to stay.

WARTS AND ALL

Debbie and I never tried to build a ministry around my experience in heaven. It was a very personal experience, and we had done all we could do to wrap our minds

113

around it. Meanwhile God orchestrated a DVD based on my appearance on CBN.[2] Truth be told, we didn't even follow the necessary steps in the requested time frame to cooperate with the idea. You could say it happened in spite of us.

During my season of searching out the why and where, I surrendered myself to Him. I said, "Lord, I leave it up to You completely. Don't let me say a word that You did not ask me to say. And don't let me fail to say anything You want me to say."

That was where I left it. Soon churches began calling and inviting me to speak. Individuals approached me and brought up the subject of heaven. I never initiated a thing. All I did was step through the doors God opened. It should not have been easy; it had never been easy for me to talk to people about the Lord. Yet once I left it in His hands, it was easy—as easy as pie.

The kicker came when a number of people said, "You need to write a book." If ever anything came at me from left field, the idea of writing a book did! I could do nothing but state the obvious: "If that idea is from God, He'll have to do it. I don't have a clue how to get it done."

Little did I know that He was doing it! When Charisma Media approached me, I explained all the reasons a book was impossible. The woman who called acknowledged my misgivings and addressed them. Still I told Debbie, "We're going to have to pray about this. Unless it's from God, I don't want it to happen."

It was from God and it did happen, but not without our having to go through a humbling process. Once we agreed to share our personal experiences, we had to decide how far we were willing to go. For Debbie and me it was all or nothing. We would not be comfortable telling our story with a coat of varnish to pretty it up. If Daddy and Mama were here, I know they would say, "Tell your story, warts and all."

GOD'S DOING

This was the LORD's doing; it is marvelous in our eyes.
—PSALM 118:23, NKJV

When I awoke to restraints in the ICU, it was the last place I wanted to be. If I could have pressed a button and been translated back to heaven, I would have pressed it without a second thought. God, however, had another plan, and I have embraced it.

There comes a point when letting go is the only thing left to do. Debbie and I have done a lot of that! He asked me to be an author, but I'm not famous. I haven't won a Nobel Prize, and I'm not a preacher or a theologian. All I have to offer is an extraordinary story about heaven, from the life of an average guy—me.

I guess that is the point. My story proves that God can use any human being, regardless of worldly qualifications and regardless of his past. His purposes are His business, and He orchestrates their fulfillment in ways that would never occur to us.

He certainly orchestrated my life, from before the

beginning to the day I died and beyond. He allowed me to experience heaven and His presence, and even now that is a privilege I find difficult to fathom. Then He sent me back so that I might bear witness to you, because He has a plan for your life too!

↙Chapter 8↘

THREE HEAVENS

You alone are the LORD; You have made
heaven, the heaven of heavens, with all their
host.... The host of heaven worships You.
NEHEMIAH 9:6, NKJV

HEAVEN IS REAL, more real than even the rodeo. I could not always have said this with such conviction. As far back as I can remember I believed with all my heart that a magnificent place called heaven existed. I liked hearing about it; I explained it to my kids; I accepted it as reality. But going there and experiencing it—well, that changed things.

It also changed me. The "human box" of my thinking was shattered. My ideas about life and death were confronted by eternity itself. There isn't a box big enough for that. Eternity explodes our human thought processes. How can we possibly wrap our minds around it while we are still here?

The truth is that we can't. We can try, but until the day comes—as mine did—we can't grasp it fully. The apostle Paul quoted the prophet Isaiah explaining how limited our human sensibilities are when it comes to the works of God:

> As it is written: "Eye has not seen, nor ear heard, nor have entered into the heart of man the things which God has prepared for those who love Him."
> —1 CORINTHIANS 2:9, NKJV

The human heart cannot understand the totality of what God has prepared. We have no reference point for it, no earthly experience to give us a clue. We know, however, that it is good. There is enough understanding in the heart of the believer, and even the unbeliever, to know that heaven is an eternal destination like no other.

Even if heaven is mysterious, it is on most people's minds. Everywhere and in most faiths, people are preoccupied by it. The place is in our spiritual DNA, whether we recognize it or not. Some of us dream about heaven. We talk about it. We write about it. We even try to pinpoint its location. We want more than anything to end up there, even though we sometimes argue about the details.

Whether or not heaven looks the way we thought it would, whether our eschatology is spot-on or way off, there is no better place than heaven. Streets of gold don't matter; gates of pearl are not the attraction. To be in heaven is to be with the Lord. That is what makes heaven perfect. He is what heaven is all about.

ONE COWBOY'S VIEW

Before I share thoughts about the three heavens, I need to lay some groundwork. Talking about heaven can lead to disagreement—about Scripture interpretation, theology, and eschatology. This book is not about any of these fields of study. I will leave the hermeneutics, doctrinal differences, and the end times to the experts. The only things I'm at all qualified or called to share are my own experiences and the things God has revealed in and through them.

Until God's eternal plan unfolds and our questions are settled forever, each of us will see things differently. That is OK with me. I believe our viewpoints are different largely based on what each of us is called to do. My understanding won't mesh perfectly with yours, and yours might not match your neighbor's. In the end He will disclose the things we cannot settle now. When that day comes, our viewpoints won't matter a lick. They will collapse under the weight of His glory, and we will see all things as they are. What a day that will be!

Along the same lines, I can share only the pieces of the puzzle that I have glimpsed. Because the picture must remain incomplete for now, the pieces might seem oddly shaped. As I have said already, I don't claim to be a theologian. I'm a cowboy who was granted a rare and cherished experience. For whatever reasons (His, not mine), God has shown me some things since He sent me back. Some of it is purely for personal consumption, to help me understand the amazing experience I had. Some is for sharing with you.

Whether the things I am about to share help to settle your heart or only challenge you to seek Him and the answers more deeply on your own, I will be satisfied that I have done what He has asked of me. Sharing the deep things of the heart has its risks. Not everyone will love what I have to say. Some will question my sense of reality. Others will wonder how I got the finer points so wrong. In the end my only desire is to please Him and to bless those to whom He sends me.

As you read, I pray you are blessed or at least provoked. What more could I ask?

THE PLACE "UP THERE"

Growing up, my idea of heaven was cobbled together from the bits and pieces I picked up here, there, and everywhere. In my mind everything I heard about heaven pointed to a mysterious place somewhere in the sky surrounded by gates of pearl. Behind those gates lived a white-haired, bearded Father God who sat on a gigantic throne and watched my every move.

My mental picture was not completely out of whack, but it was oversimplified at best. When God answered my question about where I went when I died, Paul's mention of the third heaven in 2 Corinthians 12 helped put everything in perspective. I knew there was more to heaven than a place built of gold and precious stones. There had to be more to it. Why else would Paul speak of the third heaven if there were only one place named heaven?

And how did my childhood ideas of heaven explain Jesus's words as recorded in the New King James Version of the Bible at Luke 17:21, where Jesus said the "kingdom of God is within you"? Again, I'm not a theologian, but I know most scholars agree that the kingdom of God and the kingdom of heaven are interchangeable terms. Parallel passages such as those in Matthew 4 and Mark 1 (see verses 17 and 15, respectively) seem to prove them right.

According to Jesus, then, the kingdom of heaven is within us. Surely He did not mean that the gates and the streets of gold are inside us. No. He was speaking of "another" heaven, a different use of the word than we understand the eternal place to be. The same is true of the third heaven Paul wrote about; it is a place we go to, not a place that is already inside us.

This is just a taste of where He took me with all this. I had lots of questions and holes in my overall understanding; He resolved most of it. That is what I am about to share—the way He gave it to me, and with the help of Scripture. His Word is 100 percent infallible. Bear with me, however, if I see some parts differently from the way you see them. In the end the only thing that will matter is going there.

THE HEAVEN WE
HOLD IN OUR HEARTS

When most of us hear the word *heaven*, we "see" preset pictures that have been stored in our minds for years. I have already mentioned some of them: pearly gates, streets of gold, and so on. This heaven is the place that is imprinted on most people's minds. I call it the first heaven.

The first heaven is the eternal heaven, the place Christians see as their final abode. Each of us has expectations of what the place will be like and how we will live there. Many misconceptions of heaven are embedded in our culture. Filmmakers have often depicted a place where residents grow wings, sit on puffs of cloud, and play tiny harps. I'm not arguing against harps or wings; I am saying that our preset ideas may not be accurate.

What we know for sure is that our eternal home will be more than we imagined. After all, Jesus is preparing it for us! He told His disciples as much two thousand years ago. He talked about His Father's house having many mansions. Whether He meant literal mansions or not, the word must have gotten everyone's attention. I know it gets mine.

> In My Father's house are many mansions; if it were not so, I would have told you. I go to prepare a place for you. And if I go and prepare a place for

you, I will come again and receive you to Myself;
that where I am, there you may be also.
—JOHN 14:2–3, NKJV

Maybe being a home builder makes me biased, but I do believe we will find literal mansions in the eternal heaven. I don't know whether they will conform to our earthly idea of mansions, but I think they will be there. Regardless of what they look like, Jesus said He was preparing a place for us, and anything He prepares is better than first-rate. Even a home builder like me will be impressed!

Jesus also promised to come again and receive us to Himself, so that we could be with Him. He has the details worked out. We don't have to arrange transportation or consult MapQuest. We don't have to wonder whether He will remember us. As long as we belong to Him, He will keep His word; He will see to it that we reach the place He has prepared.

If you are like me, you carry other mental pictures of heaven. One of mine involves God's throne. I think of it as being the very center of heaven. Scripture describes it somewhat, along with the rest of the first heaven. Yet not everything is revealed to us. I suppose if it were, there would be no faith involved in our future hopes.

The apostle John was permitted to see heaven when he received the Revelation of Jesus Christ. His description in chapter 4 of the Book of Revelation is more than stunning; it is earthshaking, and I suspect the place is even more amazing than his description can convey.

John's view into heaven began when he saw through an open door and heard a voice like a trumpet saying, "Come up here, and I will show you what must take place after this" (Rev. 4:1).

Talk about an invitation! Just reading about it takes my breath away. So does John's description of what he was allowed to witness. It depicts a more awesome scene than I have observed in any film:

> At once I was in the Spirit, and there before me was a throne in heaven with someone sitting on it. And the one who sat there had the appearance of jasper and ruby. A rainbow that shone like an emerald encircled the throne. Surrounding the throne were twenty-four other thrones, and seated on them were twenty-four elders. They were dressed in white and had crowns of gold on their heads. From the throne came flashes of lightning, rumblings and peals of thunder. In front of the throne, seven lamps were blazing. These are the seven spirits of God.
> —REVELATION 4:2–5

John's view of the throne room is powerful and a bit intimidating. Imagine a rainbow that shines like an emerald, even as lightning erupts and thunder rumbles from the throne! In verse 6 John describes "a sea of glass, clear as crystal" that is laid out before the throne. He then reveals "four living creatures, each having six wings...full of eyes around and within" (Rev. 4:8, NKJV).

The beauty and unearthliness revealed in John's picture of heaven are a far cry from puffy clouds and harp players.

The Old Testament prophet Daniel described heaven in a passage that parallels John's testimony. What Daniel saw is equally dramatic:

> As I looked, thrones were set in place, and the Ancient of Days took his seat. His clothing was as white as snow; the hair of his head was white like wool. His throne was flaming with fire, and its wheels were all ablaze. A river of fire was flowing, coming out from before him. Thousands upon thousands attended him; ten thousand times ten thousand stood before him. The court was seated, and the books were opened.
> —DANIEL 7:9–10

The sights John and Daniel describe are awesome in every sense of the word. So are the sounds captured in John's account:

> Day and night [the four living creatures] never stop saying: "'Holy, holy, holy is the LORD God Almighty,' who was, and is, and is to come." Whenever the living creatures give glory, honor and thanks to him who sits on the throne and who lives for ever and ever, the twenty-four elders fall down before him who sits on the throne and worship him who lives for ever and ever. They lay their crowns before the throne and say: "You are worthy, our Lord and God,

> to receive glory and honor and power, for you
> created all things, and by your will they were
> created and have their being."
> —REVELATION 4:8–11

The four living creatures and the twenty-four elders
know how to worship! Worship is what they do in the
eternal heaven. This is part of my mental picture of the
place: unending, unrestrained, unself-conscious worship.
It lines up with my own experience in the third heaven
in the sense that while I was there Jesus consumed my
attention. He was everything, and His lordship saturated
everything. So I am not surprised that worship is con-
tinuous and unabashed in the first heaven. The place is
about Him, and He is worthy of worship without end.

In later chapters of the Book of Revelation John
describes the New Jerusalem that will come out from
heaven. A. R. Fausset calls it "the eternal and consum-
mated kingdom of God on the new earth."[1] Many familiar
views of the eternal heaven come from this text. Two are
described in a single verse: "The twelve gates were twelve
pearls, each gate made of a single pearl. The great street
of the city was of gold, as pure as transparent glass"
(Rev. 21:21).

Wow, is all I can say! Even the oil-rich kingdoms of the
East cannot approximate the lavishness John described.
Yet much of what is good about our eternal abode
involves what is not there. Certain features are either
unneeded or unwanted. We will be glad to do without
them in heaven.

No Temple, Lights, Night, or Impurity

In Revelation 21 John explains how all-encompassing and complete our God is and how perfect our eternal abode will be:

> I did not see a temple in the city, because the Lord God Almighty and the Lamb are its temple. The city does not need the sun or the moon to shine on it, for the glory of God gives it light, and the Lamb is its lamp. The nations will walk by its light, and the kings of the earth will bring their splendor into it. On no day will its gates ever be shut, for there will be no night there. The glory and honor of the nations will be brought into it. Nothing impure will ever enter it, nor will anyone who does what is shameful or deceitful, but only those whose names are written in the Lamb's book of life.
> —REVELATION 21:22–27

No temple building, no light generated from without—just the Lord God Almighty, the Lamb, and their glory. The brilliance of the place will force our memories of earthly "glory" to fade.

When I was sent back to the earth and returned to my natural body, I immediately felt pain and disappointment. I was back in my broken body and it hurt. My mind grappled with my physical condition, placing a drag on my emotions.

What a far cry from heaven it was. While I was with Jesus, I had no body and no physical suffering. I experienced total life—pain, sorrow, crying, and all forms of death were quenched. It was—and it will be again—glorious!

> God himself will be with them and be their God. "He will wipe every tear from their eyes. There will be no more death" or mourning or crying or pain, for the old order of things has passed away.
> —REVELATION 21:3–4

Can you imagine a more wonderful life than the one John wrote about? Can you imagine a better ending for your loved ones?

NO HUNGER, NO THIRST, NO TEARS

Earlier in the Book of Revelation John writes that he heard one of the twenty-four elders describe the final rest of a group of believers who will suffer greatly on this earth. These are the Christians who will enter heaven after experiencing the Tribulation.

For these dear souls life will be very hard, and dying will be a great relief. Their final days will be unbearable, but because they call Christ their Savior and Lord, they will look forward to living in eternity with Him, knowing their suffering will soon be forgotten. The rest they will enjoy in heaven will wipe it all away.

The elder's words to John are some of the most comforting I can imagine hearing:

He who sits on the throne will shelter them with his presence. "Never again will they hunger; never again will they thirst. The sun will not beat down on them," nor any scorching heat. For the Lamb at the center of the throne will be their shepherd; "he will lead them to springs of living water." "And God will wipe away every tear from their eyes."

—REVELATION 7:15–17

Regardless of when we enter heaven, those of us who call Jesus our Lord and Savior will enjoy the same beautiful ease as the Tribulation sufferers. No hunger, thirst, scorching heat, or sorrow will touch us there. No need will go unmet. No regret will plague us. We will not seek respite because nothing untoward is found there. Every demand of this world and of our physical bodies will be removed. The Lamb will refresh us, and God will wipe away every tear. "God's dwelling place is now among the people, and he will dwell with them. They will be his people, and God himself will be with them and be their God" (Rev. 21:3).

Friend, heaven is real and far better than we know! When we get there, every question and form of confusion and misunderstanding will be resolved forever. "Now we see only a reflection as in a mirror; then we shall see face to face. Now I know in part; then I shall know fully, even as I am fully known" (1 Cor. 13:12). We will know fully and be fully known, and we will not be ashamed of anything.

I must say it again—if Jesus is your Lord, dying is

easy. Even your best days in this life cannot compare to eternity with Him.

THE SECOND HEAVEN— THE KINGDOM WITHIN

Heaven is not just a place but a kingdom. Remember that the kingdom of God and the kingdom of heaven are one and the same. It is an imperishable kingdom, the believer's spiritual inheritance, as Paul explained: "I declare to you, brothers and sisters, that flesh and blood cannot inherit the kingdom of God, nor does the perishable inherit the imperishable" (1 Cor. 15:50). Elsewhere Paul explained that "the kingdom of God is not a matter of eating and drinking, but of righteousness, peace and joy in the Holy Spirit" (Rom. 14:17).

This is what I see as the second heaven, the kingdom mentioned earlier that is inside the born-again believer. A physical kingdom could not exist inside a man, woman, or child, but our spiritual inheritance, God's kingdom, the kingdom of heaven does. How amazing is that?

Jesus spoke of this kingdom when religious leaders questioned Him:

> Now when He was asked by the Pharisees when the kingdom of God would come, He answered them and said, "The kingdom of God does not come with observation; nor will they say, 'See here!' or 'See there!' For indeed, the kingdom of God is within you."
> —LUKE 17:20–21, NKJV

Heaven is within us because He lives within us. We talk about "drawing near to God," but how can we be far from the One who lives inside us? What more profound privilege could there be than to be indwelt by the living God?

In a short parable Jesus explained how completely the kingdom of heaven affects us, saying, "The kingdom of heaven is like yeast that a woman took and mixed into about sixty pounds of flour until it worked all through the dough" (Matt. 13:33). Sixty pounds of flour is a lot of flour! Even so, just a small amount of yeast affects all of it.

The kingdom has the same effect on us. Once it is within us, we cannot help but be changed. The kingdom— His presence within us—changes everything.

The scribes and Pharisees were uncomfortable with the change Jesus represented. Therefore, they challenged Him in the hope of discrediting Him. One of their favorite tactics was to ask trick questions. On one occasion they asked which commandment was the most important. As always Jesus's answer shut them down. One scribe ceded the defeat and agreed with what Jesus said:

> "Well said, teacher," the man replied. "You are right in saying that God is one and there is no other but him. To love him with all your heart, with all your understanding and with all your strength, and to love your neighbor as yourself is more important than all burnt offerings and sacrifices."
>
> When Jesus saw that he had answered wisely,

> he said to him, "You are not far from the kingdom
> of God." And from then on no one dared ask him
> any more questions.
>
> —MARK 12:32–34

The scribe was not born again. Nobody was, because Jesus had not yet died and risen again. Whether the man spoke from his heart or tried to say the "the right thing," what he said was true. He described the heart of the believer, and Jesus commended his response, saying, "You are not far from the kingdom of God." He wasn't saying that the scribe was close to a physical place. Jesus was affirming His own truth.

The second heaven is the sweet and powerful communion we are invited to have with Jesus in this life. It is a taste of heaven on earth. Of course, when we die and enter our eternal rest, our fellowship will continue, but it will be seamless and unbroken, like the perfect rest I described in chapter 5. In heaven my fellowship with Jesus could not be interrupted or compromised in any way. Even if He welcomed thousands of people to heaven at the same moment that He received me, our fellowship was unaffected. He did not "subtract" from me in order to "add" to them.

Life with Jesus after death is perfect. Our fellowship with Him in this life is imperfect. Our choices and actions affect our experience of it. We can give ourselves to the kingdom of heaven within us, or we can resist. Often we resist without realizing what we have done. At other times we knowingly opt out.

Do you remember the conversation Jesus had with a rich man? The man was obviously drawn to Jesus. He asked, "Good Teacher, what shall I do that I may inherit eternal life?" (Mark 10:17, NKJV).

Jesus's answer was designed to help the man "locate" himself spiritually. Jesus listed several commandments as though to test the man's compliance. The man proudly answered that he had followed all the commandments Jesus mentioned since his youth.

Knowing that obedience was not the root issue, Jesus addressed the man's real needs. Jesus told him to sell his stuff and "follow Me." The man could not do what Jesus asked. Instead, he walked away dejected. What Jesus offered was fellowship with Him. When the man declined the offer, Jesus explained to His disciples the obstacle the man faced:

> "How hard it is for those who have riches to enter the kingdom of God!" And the disciples were astonished at His words. But Jesus answered again and said to them, "Children, how hard it is for those who trust in riches to enter the kingdom of God! It is easier for a camel to go through the eye of a needle than for a rich man to enter the kingdom of God."
> —MARK 10:23–25, NKJV

Jesus was not suggesting that a rich man cannot go to heaven. He was explaining that a rich man can become so entangled with his affairs (his business, family, wealth management, and so on) that he finds it difficult to give himself to fellowship with the Lord. His wealth does not make him evil or spiritually disqualify him—not at all. But unlike the poor person who recognizes his or her need for God, the wealthy person may not sense the urgency. He or she may find it more difficult to lay aside pressing issues and commune with the Holy Spirit.

Jesus made the kingdom within us possible. He also gave us the keys to this kingdom. He explained this to Peter after asking the disciple a pointed question about the Messiah's identity:

> "But what about you?" [Jesus] asked. "Who do you say I am?" Simon Peter answered, "You are the Christ, the Son of the living God." Jesus replied, "Blessed are you, Simon son of Jonah, for this was not revealed to you by flesh and blood, but by my Father in heaven. And I tell you that you are Peter, and on this rock I will build my church, and the gates of Hades will not overcome it. I will give you the keys of the kingdom of heaven; whatever you bind on earth will be bound in heaven, and whatever you loose on earth will be loosed in heaven."
>
> —MATTHEW 16:15–19

Peter's answer demonstrated what God had revealed. The revelation was a big deal, and Jesus made sure Peter and his peers knew how big it was. I doubt that any of the men grasped the full meaning of Jesus's response until after He ascended to the Father's right hand in the eternal heaven.

In my opinion Jesus was giving them advance notice that the rock would be the family of God—the church, the body of Christ. It was an important piece of the puzzle that would make sense to them after the Day of Pentecost, the day when Peter and his peers entered the kingdom of heaven!

Like the disciples, we learn in stages, so the Lord deals with us the way we deal with our children. He starts by giving us small puzzles with large pieces, and He gives us plenty of time to figure out where the pieces fit. At some point in our maturity we graduate to complicated, thousand-piece puzzles that require more skill and insight to complete.

The more we commune with Him, the more understanding He imparts to us. It does not come in one day or one year; He gives it incrementally as we walk with Him. He is faithful to give us the keys of the kingdom within.

THE THIRD HEAVEN, PARADISE

We touched briefly on Paul's experience in the third heaven. We will do so again here, but we will also look at two other important stories involving the third heaven.

Paul

In chapter 7 I shared a little about the third heaven and how the Lord revealed to me that this was the place I visited when I died. He led me to a passage in 2 Corinthians in which Paul describes his own experience in the third heaven. Let's take another look at the passage:

> I know a man in Christ who fourteen years ago was caught up to the third heaven. Whether it was in the body or out of the body I do not know—God knows. And I know that this man—whether in the body or apart from the body I do not know, but God knows—was caught up to paradise and heard inexpressible things, things that no one is not permitted to tell.
>
> —2 CORINTHIANS 12:2–4

Paul made it clear that the third heaven is the same place we call paradise. It is an awesome resting place, but it is not the believer's final resting place. Our eternal home—and Paul's—is the first heaven. When the Rapture occurs, the eternal heaven will be opened. Those of us who died beforehand will be reunited with our resurrected bodies and caught up into the air with Jesus. Those of us who are living on the earth at that time will be caught up immediately afterward. (See 1 Thessalonians 4:15–17.) All of us will enter the eternal heaven.

Until the Rapture occurs, believers will find their rest in the third heaven, or paradise.

Jesus

Jesus mentioned paradise as He hung on the cross next to two criminals who were crucified with Him. In the thick of their agony they had an unforgettable conversation:

One of the criminals who hung there hurled insults at [Jesus]: "Aren't you the Messiah? Save yourself and us!" But the other criminal rebuked him. "Don't you fear God," he said, "since you are under the same sentence? We are punished justly, for we are getting what our deeds deserve. But this man has done nothing wrong." Then he said, "Jesus, remember me when you come into your kingdom." Jesus answered him, "Truly I tell you, today you will be with me in paradise."

—LUKE 23:39–43

The first criminal doubted Jesus's identity as the Messiah, but not the second criminal. He recognized who Jesus was, and he wanted to be with Him in eternity. Imagine his joy when Jesus promised that they would meet again in paradise that very day!

Jesus knew ahead of time where He was going. Like any other human being who dies, His earthly body would stay behind when His spirit departed. That moment came when "Jesus called out with a loud voice, 'Father, into your hands I commit my spirit.' When he had said this, he breathed his last" (Luke 23:46).

When Jesus released His spirit into God's hands, He went to the third heaven. His body and His mind were left behind, hanging on the cross. Soon the centurions took down His battered corpse, and it was laid in a tomb. That is where His body and mind remained until the third day, when Jesus was resurrected and reunited with His spirit.

This is a picture of what will happen when our spirits are reunited with our bodies at the Rapture. Jesus Christ, "the firstborn from the dead" (Rev. 1:5), foreshadowed it for us.

Stephen

Stephen was one of the first seven men chosen as deacons in the early church. He was a bold witness for Christ whose testimony inflamed the religious leaders of his day. The claims of the Messiah and His followers threatened the status quo in Israel. Those holding religious power feared their claims and their passion for Jesus.

Stephen never balked at the price of his faith and ministry. Even when Jewish leaders accused him of blasphemy, false witnesses testified against him, and the Sanhedrin questioned him, he professed Christ. When the high priest asked Stephen whether he had testified publicly about Jesus the Messiah, the disciple could have cowered and saved his own neck. Instead, Stephen admitted his zeal! Not only did he mention Jesus Christ but he also outlined the Jews' entire history.

Stephen's audacity infuriated his seething audience. How they reacted was no surprise:

> When the members of the Sanhedrin heard this, they were furious and gnashed their teeth at him. But Stephen, full of the Holy Spirit, looked up to heaven and saw the glory of God, and Jesus standing at the right hand of God. "Look," he said, "I see heaven open and the Son of Man standing at the right hand of God."

At this they covered their ears and, yelling at the top of their voices, they all rushed at him, dragged him out of the city and began to stone him. Meanwhile, the witnesses laid their coats at the feet of a young man named Saul.

While they were stoning him, Stephen prayed, "Lord Jesus, receive my spirit." Then he fell on his knees and cried out, "Lord, do not hold this sin against them." When he had said this, he fell asleep.

—ACTS 7:54–60

In biblical language falling asleep is dying. Stephen became the first Christian martyr that day. Saul, who later became the apostle Paul, fiercely persecuted Christians at that time, and he watched Stephen's death with great satisfaction. Ironically, Stephen the deacon went to the third heaven even before Paul the Apostle believed Jesus was the Messiah!

With Stephen dead and Christians aware of the danger they faced, "Saul began to destroy the church. Going from house to house, he dragged off men and women and put them in prison" (Acts 8:3). Stephen's death began a long season of persecution. The first martyr and those who followed gave their lives willingly.

Take another look at Luke's account in Acts. It describes Stephen's frame of mind just before the stoning began:

But Stephen, full of the Holy Spirit, looked up to heaven and saw the glory of God, and Jesus standing at the right hand of God. "Look," he said, "I see heaven open and the Son of Man standing at the right hand of God."

—ACTS 7:55–56

I believe every martyr faces a moment of reckoning. Stephen could dread his fate, or he could embrace his final mission. Being full of the Holy Spirit, he saw God's big picture, and it was all he needed to see. He knew dying would be easy. He knew God and his eternal home awaited him. I believe he saw the purpose of his earthly life reaching fulfillment in God's timing and was happy to wrap up his work and go on to his reward.

YOU AND ME

The third heaven is a wondrous place of intimate and ultimate fellowship with Jesus Christ. It thrills me to know that every believer this side of the Rapture will enjoy it.

I am not advocating anyone's premature death or the view of heaven as an escape hatch. Each of us has work to do here and a set time to go home. But to those whose hearts are breaking because of a terminal diagnosis given to them or to a loved one, I can promise you that you will not arrive in paradise feeling that you have been shortchanged—only rewarded early.

If I die again before the Rapture, I know I will return to paradise. The same is true for every Christian. Then, when Jesus comes for His church, those of us in paradise and those who are still alive on the earth will be gathered according to the plan laid out in Scripture:

According to the Lord's word, we tell you that we who are still alive, who are left until the coming of the Lord, will certainly not precede those who have fallen asleep. For the Lord himself will come down from heaven, with a loud command, with the voice of the archangel and with the trumpet call of God, and the dead in Christ will rise first. After that, we who are still alive and are left will be caught up together with them in the clouds to meet the Lord in the air. And so we will be with the Lord forever. Therefore encourage each other with these words.

—1 THESSALONIANS 4:15–18

Those already deceased will be gathered first. Not only will they rise but they will also be reunited with their bodies, which will be glorified, immortal bodies without blemish, as Paul explained:

But our citizenship is in heaven. And we eagerly await a Savior from there, the Lord Jesus Christ, who, by the power that enables him to bring everything under his control, will transform our lowly bodies so that they will be like his glorious body.

—PHILIPPIANS 3:20–21

I believe the day is coming when the saints of God will stand in white robes at God's throne watching Jesus and His angels defeat Satan and his cohorts. Satan will be bound, and we will reign on earth with the Messiah for one thousand years.

Paul told us to encourage one another by talking about these events (see 1 Thessalonians 4:18). I pray my discussion about them encourages you! If you have already accepted Christ's finished work, it will. If not, I am inviting you again—He is inviting you again—to make that eternal decision with a simple prayer:

> *Jesus, I repent of my sins and I receive You as my Savior and Lord. I believe that You died for my sake, to cleanse me of all sin. Thank You for Your precious sacrifice and for making me a new creation. Amen.*

⸺Chapter 9⸺

ETERNITY in US

*He has made everything beautiful in its time. He has
also set eternity in the human heart; yet no one can
fathom what God has done from beginning to end.*
ECCLESIASTES 3:11

AFTER MY VISIT to heaven God showed me new
things (at least they were new to me) about how
He created us to function. I knew that physical
death forced my spirit, mind, and body to part. Only
my spirit went to be with Him, which says a lot about
how important the spirit is. What He shared helped me
to understand how important. It also brought the big
picture—and I mean really big—into better focus.

He showed me something else too—something unexpected. I call it the timeline. Like everything else He
reveals, the timeline has forever changed my approach
to eternity and everyday life. It is one of those things He
gave me to share. Few people take a preliminary visit to
heaven; sharing what I learned from mine is part of the
reason He returned me to this life. Like everything else

He asks me to do, it will accomplish His will because it is His idea, not mine.

Let me first repeat my disclaimer: I'm not a theologian. You may wonder why I keep saying it. The reason is that I am not called to teach anybody about religion. I don't know anything about religion. All I know is what He shows me in His Word, what He speaks to my heart, and what obedience looks like in my life. I am not a preacher but a cowboy called to comfort others with the comfort that has comforted me. I will put the ideas in human language the best I can and trust His Holy Spirit to fill in the blanks.

> Praise be to the God and Father of our Lord Jesus Christ, the Father of compassion and the God of all comfort, who comforts us in all our troubles, so that we can comfort those in any trouble with the comfort we ourselves receive from God.
> —2 CORINTHIANS 1:3–4

THE UNGRASPABLE ETERNAL

God's timeline is eternity. I know that sounds like a given, but it is also a mystery. How can a human mind grasp the idea? Can we truly envision something that has no beginning and no end?

The answer is yes and no. I already described the no part. The yes is found in Scripture. Solomon wrote that eternity is in our hearts (Eccles. 3:11). God made us in His image and likeness, so eternity is in our hearts. We know that we know that our God and His kingdom are eternal. Even so, the concept boggles our minds.

Maybe it is just me, but have you ever tried to comprehend the idea of an eternal God? I'm not talking about believing it. We Christians believe it by faith; we believe God is, and we believe He is eternal. But I don't know any human being who can explain a being who has no beginning and no end, who always was and always will be. It is like trying to understand how far the universe reaches and wondering what is on the other side of its boundaries.

Trying to figure out these things makes my head hurt. Maybe it does yours too. I cannot speak for everyone, but it is safe to say that human beings do better with finiteness. We get that. We understand time in a linear way; we know the clock ticks 86,400 times each day. We spend a lot of time "watching the clock" because we know that time "runs out." We mete out the hours as carefully as we can so we keep our commitments, meet our deadlines, get enough rest, and do the things we enjoy doing with loved ones.

But eternity? It is difficult to describe without experiencing it. Even then words fall short.

Solomon had the God-given insight to say that eternity is in our hearts. It is almost ironic then that one of his best-known contributions to the biblical canon is about time. In the famous passage in Ecclesiastes, he did what we do. He connected time with human activity:

> There is a time for everything, and a season for
> every activity under the heavens: a time to be
> born and a time to die, a time to plant and a
> time to uproot, a time to kill and a time to heal,
> a time to tear down and a time to build, a time
> to weep and a time to laugh, a time to mourn
> and a time to dance, a time to scatter stones and
> a time to gather them, a time to embrace and a
> time to refrain from embracing, a time to search
> and a time to give up, a time to keep and a time
> to throw away, a time to tear and a time to mend,
> a time to be silent and a time to speak, a time
> to love and a time to hate, a time for war and a
> time for peace.
> —ECCLESIASTES 3:1–8

Humans are more often time conscious than eternity conscious, so Solomon's poetic "calendar" rings true. We do certain things at certain times because we know those times are better than others. To keep it all straight, we make distinctions about what is past, present, and future. We say, "I was born on such and such a day," or "I am laughing," or "I will scatter stones tomorrow."

For God it is different. He reigns in all eternity simultaneously, including what we would call the future. He set eternity in motion and is master of it. Nothing in or about time controls Him, makes Him nervous, or changes His mind. Eternity is what is, and we are in it. Each day we watch the unfolding of what He already established.

Solomon talked about that too:

> I know that everything God does will endure
> forever; nothing can be added to it and nothing
> taken from it.... Whatever is has already been,
> and what will be has been before; and God will
> call the past to account.
>
> —Ecclesiastes 3:14–15

God is eternal, unchanging, and in charge.

In His Image

God made us—at least part of us—to be eternal. When He created Adam, He said, "Let us make mankind in our image, in our likeness" (Gen. 1:26). When He said "our image" He was talking about the Trinity: the Father, the Son, and the Holy Spirit. Because the triune God made mankind in His image, we also have three parts—not Father, Son, and Holy Spirit, but mind, body, and spirit. In Bible terminology we are tripartite beings.

Spirit

When I went to heaven only my spirit, the eternal part of me, went. My body and mind stayed behind. Had God not dispatched my spirit from heaven, my abandoned parts would have decayed and become earth dust. I did not need them in heaven. They were not the "real me" anyway. They were the shell that carried the real me while I lived in the physical, earthly realm.

That is the point: My earthly life was and is temporary. I was created first and foremost as a spirit being, and so were you!

By God's design Freddy Vest, the spirit being, lives in an earthly body, at least for now. When I accepted salvation at the age of eleven, my spirit was made alive again. This is the most important part of me. In terms of the Trinity my spirit corresponds to the Holy Spirit Jesus promised would come after He ascended to the right hand of the Father (see John 14:26). My spirit is not on the same level as the Holy Spirit, but it does reflect the image of God. It is all I need to commune with Him.

In heaven Jesus and I communicated without thinking or using words. We instantly understood each other, without any chance of misunderstanding. My human spirit will go to heaven again someday, but it communicates with God even now, while I am in my physical body. The communication is not as seamless as it was in heaven, but my spirit still learns from Him. Then it sends what He says to my mind, so I can act on it.

Body

Jesus needed a body to live on earth, and so do I. My body is the part that corresponds to the second member of the Trinity—Jesus, the all-giving Lord, who came in the flesh.

Using my body, I can work, serve others, and procreate according to God's eternal plan. My body allows me to do His bidding on the earth. Dominion is a key aspect of His will, and it is tied to His image:

> Then God said, "Let Us make man in Our image, according to Our likeness; let them have

dominion over the fish of the sea, over the birds of the air, and over the cattle, over all the earth and over every creeping thing that creeps on the earth."

—GENESIS 1:26, NKJV

Our bodies allow us to function in the earth, the dust from which God made the first human body—Adam's body. God did not stop at the dust; He gave life to Adam with His own breath. How powerful it is to read about it again!

The LORD God formed a man from the dust of the ground and breathed into his nostrils the breath of life, and the man became a living being.

—GENESIS 2:7

Mind

For my body to do God's will, my mind must work. It is the part of me that corresponds to God the Father, the source of all knowledge. My mind is not all-knowing like He is, but He fashioned it so I could know and learn.

My mind includes my thought processes. They are an important part of my life. When I was eleven, I had already thought about salvation many times. On the day I finally answered the altar call, my mind had a role in my decision. It was involved in the exercise of my will to say yes to Christ.

My mind—more specifically, my brain—has a physical role in telling my body what to do. When I want to mount my horse, my brain sends signals to my body so it can obey. No sooner do I think about riding than I have one foot in a stirrup and another leg swinging over my mount.

The human mind is amazing—and powerful! God created it that way. Yet speaking for myself (and Scripture will bear me out), if I leave my mind to its own devices, it will get crosswise of God in a New York minute.

My natural thoughts run contrary to His image in me. They lean toward fear and selfishness and other worldly ways that oppose Him and the real me—my spirit. My mind will yield to my spirit, but only if it is continually renewed. Then I will "prove what is that good and acceptable and perfect will of God" (Rom. 12:2, NKJV).

In this physical life my mind and body make many demands of me. If I let them, they will hog my attention and draw me away from God. That has happened more times than I care to admit.

Thankfully it does not happen in heaven—ever. When my earthly body died and my spirit was free, there were no distractions—no pains, no wants, and no worries to interfere. Not only that, but I "conversed" with Jesus 100 percent on His terms. The filters that play into earthly communication were gone; He had my undivided and untainted attention.

This is what you and I were created for! We are not bodies that happen to have spirits inside. We are spirit beings who happen to live in flesh-and-blood bodies!

God made us the way He did so we could be like Him and communicate intimately with Him. We live on the earth in physical bodies for however many years He grants us. Our bodies serve their purposes but are temporary. The spirit goes on eternally (in heaven, if we choose Christ).

After going to heaven I realized how much care I'd given to my body and my mind, often at the cost of my spirit. I actually neglected my spirit—the very part that connects with Him. I still take care of my body and my mind, but now that I understand the importance of my spirit, I take much better care of it.

THE TRIPARTITE JESUS

Another thing I have learned since returning from heaven might seem obvious. Yet it is easy to overlook. It is the tripartite nature of Jesus.

Of course, Jesus is the second person of the Trinity, but He also lived on the earth as a human being who had a spirit, mind, and body as every human does. I am not talking here about the Holy Spirit, the third person of the Trinity. I am talking about the spirit that left Jesus's body when He breathed His last on the cross.

In the Garden of Gethsemane Jesus knew He would soon take the sin of the entire world on Himself and pay the death penalty for it. He prayed, "Take this cup from me. Yet not what I will, but what you will" (Mark 14:36).

As He prayed fervently, His disciples slept. Jesus understood their lapse, but He warned them just the same, saying, "Watch and pray so that you will not fall into temptation. The spirit is willing, but the flesh is weak" (v. 38).

We easily assume that Jesus was referring to their weaknesses alone, but He understood human weakness firsthand. The Book of Hebrews says that He experienced everything we experience, so that we now have an Advocate who can relate to us: "For we do not have a high priest who is unable to empathize with our weaknesses, but we have one who has been tempted in every way, just as we are—yet he did not sin" (Heb. 4:15).

Jesus knows the human struggle inside and out. He experienced the conflict between the spirit and the flesh of a man. He also acknowledged the separation of the two in death. From the cross He said, "Father, into your hands I commit my spirit." The Bible tells us "when he had said this, he breathed his last" (Luke 23:46). The spirit Jesus released at that moment was not the Holy Spirit, but the spirit of Jesus, the Man. When the Man died, His spirit went to the third heaven.

TRIPARTITE BALANCE

God made Adam and Eve as tripartite beings in the image and likeness of God. There is no imbalance in the Godhead. There is no tug of war among Father, Son, and Holy Spirit. Adam and Eve (created in His image) enjoyed perfect health and perfect balance—spirit, mind, and body.

It did not last. The serpent deceived Adam and Eve, and they took the bait. From that moment on the balance they had known was thrown off kilter. It remains volatile to this day:

> [Eve] also gave some [of the fruit] to her hus-
> band, who was with her, and he ate it. Then the
> eyes of both of them were opened, and they real-
> ized they were naked.... Then the man and his
> wife heard the sound of the LORD God as he was
> walking in the garden in the cool of the day, and
> they hid from the LORD God among the trees
> of the garden. But the LORD God called to the
> man, "Where are you?" He answered, "I heard
> you in the garden, and I was afraid because I was
> naked; so I hid."
>
> —GENESIS 3:6–10

Instead of communing in peace with the Spirit of God, Adam and Eve allowed their minds to be entangled with fear. Their bodies followed their minds down the same dark alley. Instead of running toward God, they avoided Him. When He reached out to them, they tried to shift the blame for their sin: Adam pointed the finger at Eve; Eve pointed at the serpent. I like to say it was the first time in history that someone passed the buck.

All kidding aside, the consequences were devastating. We are still dealing with them today. Satan works the system to deceive us. He does it the same way he did then: he goes after our minds, including our emotions. He incites insecurities and then works them to under-mine our trust in God. He stirs cravings for things God warned us to avoid. If we bite, we end up with something we never needed in the first place.

That is what happened in the garden. Satan engaged Eve's flesh. She surrendered to his demonic suggestion and passed the plate to her husband, who jumped at the opportunity. At that point the flesh took ascendancy over the spirit. If I were to draw a diagram to illustrate the imbalance, I would trace a circle the size of a fifty-cent piece to represent the flesh. A quarter-sized circle would picture the mind. The smallest circle, about the size of a dime, would show the neglected spirit. That is not a good balance!

Having spirit, mind, and body balanced does not mean eliminating the last two. God does not ask us to boycott mind or body. They are part of His design. As long as we are walking this earth, we need both of them, and we need to use them well. Balance comes when we consider and "consult" the spirit first—the spirit within us and the Holy Spirit. Keeping the spirit above the mind and body brings the mind and body in line.

The apostle Paul was very familiar with the battle for balance. The seventh chapter of the Book of Romans describes it in brutally honest detail. Paul wrote often about maintaining balance. His entire ministry demonstrated what he learned. He instructed, "Put on the Lord Jesus Christ, and make no provision for the flesh, to fulfill its lusts" (Rom. 13:14, NKJV). He gave a key for denying the flesh the upper hand:

> Offer your bodies as a living sacrifice, holy and pleasing to God—this is your true and proper worship. Do not conform to the pattern of this world, but be transformed by the renewing of your mind. Then you will be able to test and

approve what God's will is—his good, pleasing and perfect will.

—Romans 12:1–2

We know the body needs nourishment to perform. But so does the mind. It needs a solid diet of the wisdom and knowledge of God to keep it working soundly. The spirit also needs to be fed—with the love of God most of all. His love is our lifeblood; it is the foundation of everything He has done for us or given us. Feeding on His love enables us to love Him and those around us. The more we open ourselves to His love, the more love we can give. As John wrote, "We love because he first loved us" (1 John 4:19).

Love is so powerful that we fulfill all the commandments when we walk in it. (See Matthew 22:37–40.) If we love others, we won't steal from them or slander or abuse them. Our love will lead us to bless and protect them and to rejoice in their well-being and their triumphs. As we love, we grow spiritually, conferring with the Holy Spirit and becoming more tender and receptive to God's ways and will. When we yield to Him, the Holy Spirit influences the spirit within us, and we become more like Him. When this balance is working, the tug of war is over.

Balance and the Second Heaven

Living with spirit, mind, and body in the right balance is a doorway to the second heaven, which is the kingdom of God within you (see Luke 17:21). The second heaven is the "place" where we commune with Him. Think about Adam and Eve in the garden. Before the Fall, they lived in unbroken communion with God. Their fellowship was unself-conscious and perfectly natural to them. They had no cares or worries. They were naked and unbothered by it. They talked with God freely and openly because they were without shame or any other interference.

But when they were tempted and allowed their minds and bodies to rule, they ignored the part of them that responded to God. They gave the upper hand to the parts that were least trustworthy—the ones that could be manipulated by Satan. Once they sinned, shame tainted them. Instead of being open with their Creator, they fled from Him. Now the One whose presence kept them secure was the One they feared. With one decision they created an obstacle that distracted them from God's presence.

If you are a parent, you have seen your children go through similar patterns. When they are little, children run to Mama and Daddy whenever they feel afraid. But when they keep an embarrassing secret or tell a lie, they end up unconsciously condemning themselves and fearing the ones who love them most—even before their parents know what they have done. Instead of receiving the comfort their parents want to give, they cut themselves off from it.

This happened to the rich man we discussed in the previous chapter. He asked Jesus how to inherit eternal life but stumbled over the answer Jesus gave him (see

Mark 10:17–22). The man was out of balance. He was so weighed down with the concerns of earthly life and wealth that he forfeited the life he obviously longed to live—a life of communion with Jesus.

The man's wealth was not the problem; his spirit, mind, and body were simply out of kilter. When he pondered Jesus's answer, the man looked to his worldly checklist instead of the eternal one. His desire was spiritual, but his focus was earthbound.

When Jesus said, "Go, sell everything you have and give to the poor, and you will have treasure in heaven. Then come, follow me" (Mark 10:21), the man searched his mind and his body for his response. His mind calculated the cost. He feared losing his wealth. He was accustomed to high living. The sacrifice seemed too much.

Divine opportunity took a backseat to what the flesh prioritized. The man ended up squandering an invitation to something much better than money. He missed an entrance to the second heaven—communion with the King of kings.

Jesus was right. "The spirit is willing, but the flesh is weak" (Matt. 26:41).

SPIRITUAL WORSHIP

The kingdom of God within us has everything to do with worship. The rich man in Mark 10 had good intentions. He did not slander Jesus or discredit His teaching, as many in his position had done. He did not mock Jesus or laugh at Him. Instead, the man showed remorse. He had asked a very important question about eternal life. In fact, it was the most important question a human being can ask.

The man probably did not realize that he worshipped his wealth more than he did the Lord. We make similar mistakes today. We don't always realize that our worship is misdirected. Even those of us who call Jesus Savior bow down to idols. We don't mean to, but we do.

This brings me back to Romans 12:1–2, this time with worship in mind:

> Therefore, I urge you, brothers and sisters, in view of God's mercy, to offer your bodies as a living sacrifice, holy and pleasing to God—this is your true and proper worship. Do not conform to the pattern of this world, but be transformed by the renewing of your mind. Then you will be able to test and approve what God's will is—his good, pleasing and perfect will.

The rich man conformed "to the pattern of this world." He lost sight of eternal things.

It is so easy to do! We try to be responsible with all God has given us; we want to give Him honor in all things. Yet we can take such good care of our affairs that we neglect our fellowship with Him. Like the rich man, we slip out of balance.

The rich man missed the opportunity for his spiritual act of worship. His mind and flesh could not agree with his becoming "a living sacrifice." That is not where his focus was, and worship is a matter of focus.

I have made the same mistake as the rich man, and I have done it enough times to know that my way needed adjusting. Now my approach is simple: I have what I call my "do-right" list. Whether I am thinking, speaking, or doing something on the job, I bring my focus back to Him. Seeing everything through that prism helps me to have the right thoughts, speak the right words, and do the right deeds.

Thinking of Jesus and seeing everything else in that context transforms me and my actions. When I'm looking at Him it is difficult to conform to the world's ways. That is my spiritual act of worship—my way of offering my body as a sacrifice to Him and renewing my mind so that God's perfect will is approved in my life.

I can promise you that I don't get this right every time, but as long as I keep my mind fixed on the Lord, my thoughts and actions tend to line up behind my spirit. Instead of having a constant battle with my flesh, I find the second heaven wide open to me—not because I did everything right but because I focused on the One who is righteousness personified.

WHEN LIFE BEGINS

Before I share the full timeline God shared with me, there are two things I need to mention. The first is a question I often asked myself before I died: When does life begin?

I realize this is an enormous issue that has bitterly divided American society. The question was not political for me; it was spiritual. I have seen the answer differently over the years. Early in my life I believed that life began the moment you were born. As I got older, I thought about it some more. The process of development inside the womb became an issue for me, and I decided that life started the instant a sperm fertilized an egg. The majority of evangelicals and many other Christians, as well as some unbelievers, agree that life begins at conception.

As it did for my view about almost everything else in my life, my trip to heaven changed my perspective about the beginning of life. In retrospect I see that it was inevitable. How could the experience of death and eternity not affect my thinking about the beginning of human life?

You may have already guessed where I'm going with this: I now believe that our lives started before the foundation of the earth. This is not purely my opinion; I believe many scriptures declare it. One of them is a powerful and well-known selection from Ephesians that lays out the personal aspect of God's eternal timeline:

> Praise be to the God and Father of our Lord Jesus Christ, who has blessed us in the heavenly realms with every spiritual blessing in Christ. For he chose us in him before the creation of the world to be holy and blameless in his sight. In love he predestined us for adoption to sonship through Jesus Christ, in accordance with his pleasure and will—to the praise of his glorious grace, which he has freely given us in the One he loves.
> —EPHESIANS 1:3–6

Before the foundations of the world—however long ago that was—He chose us! That is a divine viewpoint difficult for any human to fully understand. Even hours before we were conceived, no human being, unless divinely inspired, could or would choose us for any-thing—not for a job or a team or an Academy Award. How could they? We had not yet entered the physical realm. Our bodies were not yet formed. There was no "us" for them to choose. Yet God chose us before the world's foundation.

Did that hit you as it did me? Well, there's more! Consider what God said to the prophet Jeremiah: "Before I formed you in the womb I knew you, before you were born I set you apart; I appointed you as a prophet to the nations" (Jer. 1:5). God set Jeremiah apart; He chose Him to be His prophet because He knew him.

God's Word is so plain: He knew Jeremiah before the prophet was conceived. But how did God know someone who, from our perspective, did not yet exist? I believe the answer is found in our tripartite nature. The real Jeremiah, the spirit part, existed in eternity with God before he was conceived. According to the passage from Ephesians, Jeremiah went even further back with God, before the world was ever made.

Paul captured similar ideas in his epistle to the Romans:

> We know that in all things God works for the good of those who love him, who have been called according to his purpose. For those God

> foreknew he also predestined to be conformed
> to the image of his Son, that he might be the
> firstborn among many brothers and sisters. And
> those he predestined, he also called; those he
> called, he also justified; those he justified, he
> also glorified.
>
> —ROMANS 8:28–30

The eternal God predestined, called, justified, and glorified us!

These passages speak to me about something besides a person's spirit being with the Lord in eternity past; they show the person's entire life being with Him too. The complete life cycle—from the spirit that is with God before the foundations of the earth, to the tripartite being that is born into the earth, to the spirit that returns to heaven, all the way to the spirit and glorified body that will reign with Christ in the millennium—all of it was known by God before He said, "Let there be light" (Gen. 1:3).

Knowing this can transform your whole life! If you grew up being told that you were "an accident," you now know that was a lie. You are the furthest thing from an accident. You are God's creation released into the earth at a time of His choosing. You were not sent here as an afterthought. Your future was predestined by Him!

If you live with the fear of death—whether you are perfectly healthy or your doctor claims your days are "numbered"—you don't need to fear death any longer. Your death is as much a part of God's unfolding eternity as your birth was. If you belong to Jesus, your death will be glorious, a far better experience even than being born. In birth you entered a fallen world filled with suffering. In death you will enter your true home, where suffering will never touch you again.

If your life has been difficult or marked by unspeakable tragedy, you can find peace knowing that the story of your earthly life is still unfolding. If you are reading these words, you are still here for a reason. In God's eyes you have more living to do, more moments to share, and more people to love. No matter how long we live on the earth, our lives have barely begun.

DESTINY AND ETERNITY

Destiny is a big topic. I can share only the parts I am called to talk about. One has to do with the way we live hour by hour. The other involves where our hearts are. Both affect destiny.

God established a destiny for each of us, but we play a part in how it unfolds. There is a saying that explains this. I did not originate the saying, but I follow it. It goes like this: a repeated thought becomes an action; a repeated action becomes a habit; a repeated habit becomes character; repeated character becomes destiny.

Everything starts with a thought! Imagine where that leads, then reflect on your thoughts today. Did you belittle yourself because you failed to do something exactly right? Did you decide that your situation in life was hopeless? Did you fear that your child would never return to the straight and narrow? Did you expect to fail in some endeavor, or do you fear failing again because you have failed in the past? Did you miss the beauty of today because you fear death? Have you habitually postponed life's joys because of your fear?

Our thoughts produce results, including action and inaction (which can be just as costly). Either way our choices eventually live up to our expectations. Here's an example. Do you remember what my Uncle Bill told me years ago? He said that if I would practice, I would be a calf roper someday.

What if Uncle Bill had said something negative instead? What if he said I was too clumsy to be a roper—and I believed it? With the clumsy label stuck in my mind I would eventually have done things that seemed to prove I was clumsy. Before long clumsiness would become a habit that would mark my character. If I dug the groove deep enough, I would create a destiny God never intended for me and wonder why in the world He let my life turn out that way.

The other part of this involves the heart on another level. I have to ask myself whether I'm dwelling on the things of God or the things of the world. I hate to pick on the rich man again, but isn't that exactly what tripped him up? He dwelled on worldly things, and it cost him. He had a face-to-face encounter with Jesus Christ and passed on the most significant opportunity of his life.

Our destinies extend beyond physical death. Do you remember what Jesus said? "In My Father's house are many mansions; if it were not so, I would have told you. I go to prepare a place for you" (John 14:2, NKJV).

What a beautiful promise that is! The eternal destiny God has in mind is a good one—the best one. He longs to welcome every person He created into the eternal heaven with Him. Hell does exist, but He did not create it for people. He sent the Savior so people wouldn't end up there.

God provided eternal life with Him, but we have to agree to accept it. We must believe on the Lord Jesus Christ. Paul explained the decision:

> If you declare with your mouth, "Jesus is Lord," and believe in your heart that God raised him from the dead, you will be saved. For it is with your heart that you believe and are justified, and it is with your mouth that you profess your faith and are saved.
> —ROMANS 10:9–10

We saw the word *justified* in a verse we read earlier: "Those he predestined, he also called; those he called, he also justified; those he justified, he also glorified" (Rom. 8:30). When you know you were chosen to be called, justified, and glorified, life's obstacles cannot stop you. Despite the turbulence you experience, your destiny will be big enough in your thinking to overshadow it. When this is your perspective, you will fulfill your destiny on the earth and in eternity. God has already prepared the way for you.

> For we are God's [own] handiwork (His workmanship), recreated in Christ Jesus, [born anew]

that we may do those good works which God predestined (planned beforehand) for us [taking paths which He prepared ahead of time], that we should walk in them [living the good life which He prearranged and made ready for us to live].

—EPHESIANS 2:10, AMP

DESTINY DESPITE IT ALL

Not long ago I received a phone call from a man I didn't know. "Are you Freddy Vest?" he asked.

"Yes, I am," I replied.

He said, "I'll try to get through this conversation without crying."

Remember, I'm the guy in the hospital who bawled a lot. I told the man, "That's OK. Cry if you need to."

He did cry, explaining that he'd been looking for me for years. He saw my video testimony[1] and it deeply affected him. I knew what was coming next. He told me he had died many years ago in a terrible car wreck and then come back to life. I won't go into the details. Suffice to say that his injuries were so severe they could have left him unable to accomplish anything.

After being unconscious for six weeks, he asked, "Am I dead?"

"You have been," was the answer.

It turns out that, except for the shooting prayers I saw, this man and I had almost identical experiences in heaven. I cannot put into words how comforting it is for people who have been there to exchange testimonies. It just is. I have done it many times now. This man had not yet shared his story with outsiders. His calling me was a big deal.

After having died, he dealt with the same questions I did. We talked about them and about God's ability to bring His plan to pass. I shared with him how I had tried at first to make things happen. It seemed to help him sort through his own calling; I am thankful it did.

Like anyone stricken by catastrophe, the man had been through a lot. Despite the trauma (both physical and otherwise), he has lived an exceptional and productive life. The accident nearly destroyed his future. But God preserved it and him. Today God uses this man's abilities to serve and empower others. His destiny is still being fulfilled.

THE TIMELINE

Finally—the timeline! It is a picture of God's eternal plan for every human being and for His church. He laid it out with six clear markers. We have already discussed some of them. Now we will tie them together.

Remember, this is not a theological or doctrinal presentation. It is just what He has given me to share with you. You might see it differently. Or some part of it might "click" as you read it. Maybe it will explain something you have always wondered about. In any case don't expect an exhaustive picture of eternity. Only He can provide that.

Your spirit before the foundation of the earth was laid

We talked about this earlier in the section "When Life Begins." God knew you before the foundation of the world. He has always known you and your purpose. The "you" I am talking about is not the physical you that the world recognizes, but the spirit, which is eternal and is known by your Creator.

Your spirit was with God before the beginning of time. Second Timothy 1:9 says, "He has saved us and called us to a holy life—not because of anything we have done but because of his own purpose and grace. This grace was given us in Christ Jesus before the beginning of time."

Your spirit at the point of conception

A question helped me to understand conception. You can ask yourself: When I was conceived, did God give me a spirit to live inside my body? Or did He create a physical body for my spirit, which already existed?

I believe the latter is accurate. Your spirit is the lasting part of you, the most important part. Your body is temporary; it comes and goes in what eternity would call the blink of an eye. Your physical body is designed for use on earth and allows you to accomplish your earthly destiny. Your spirit lives in your body. Once you accept Christ's sacrifice and are saved, the Holy Spirit comes to live in you and commune with your spirit. Paul said it this way: "Don't you know that you yourselves are God's temple and that God's Spirit dwells in your midst?" (1 Cor. 3:16).

Your physical death

When your body dies, your spirit makes its exit instantly. If you have accepted the salvation Jesus Christ purchased for you at Calvary (and you die before the Rapture occurs), the real you—your spirit—will enter paradise immediately. This is the third heaven, the resting place I visited; the one you and I "visited" together in earlier chapters.

I believe that, from the time of Adam to the death of Christ, the spirits of those who died were held at rest in their graves. A scriptural example comes to mind. It was when Jesus spoke about those who were already dead and buried. He said, "a time is coming when all who are in their graves will hear his voice and come out—those who have done what is good will rise to live, and those who have done what is evil will rise to be condemned" (John 5:28–29).

Peter described how, at His death, Jesus ministered to those held captive in their graves:

> Christ also suffered once for sins, the righteous for the unrighteous, to bring you to God. He was put to death in the body but made alive in the Spirit. After being made alive, he went and made proclamation to the imprisoned spirits.
> —1 PETER 3:18–19

After Christ was crucified, He preached to the spirits in prison! He then ascended and led the captives in his train to the third heaven, paradise. Psalm 68:18

says: "When you ascended on high, you took many captives." Ephesians 4:8 appears to be quoting the psalmist's record: "When he ascended on high, he took many captives." Christ freed the spirits from their graves and gave them rest, love, and comfort in paradise, where all spirits will remain until the Rapture takes place.

The Rapture

At the Rapture Jesus will descend from heaven and gather two groups of His people. First, the bodies of those who already died (and called Christ Savior) will be resurrected from their graves, reunited with their spirits, and caught up with Him in the air. Next, all believers who are still alive will rise to meet Him in the air.

Imagine what a day that will be for the church! Paul described it:

> According to the Lord's own word, we tell you that we who are still alive, who are left till the coming of the Lord, will certainly not precede those who have fallen asleep. For the Lord himself will come down from heaven, with a loud command, with the voice of the archangel and with the trumpet call of God, and the dead in Christ will rise first. After that, we who are still alive and are left will be caught up together with them in the clouds to meet the Lord in the air. And so we will be with the Lord forever.
>
> —1 THESSALONIANS 4:15–17

Both groups will also receive their glorified bodies (as Jesus's body is already glorified). Paul also described the changing of our bodies from mortal, earthly vessels to imperishable, glorified bodies:

> Listen, I tell you a mystery: We will not all sleep, but we will all be changed—in a flash, in the twinkling of an eye, at the last trumpet. For the trumpet will sound, the dead will be raised imperishable, and we will be changed. For the perishable must clothe itself with the imperishable, and the mortal with immortality. When the perishable has been clothed with the imperishable, and the mortal with immortality, then the saying that is written will come true: "Death has been swallowed up in victory."
>
> —1 Corinthians 15:51–54

From the Rapture forward God's people will worship at His throne. From the throne room they will watch as Jesus and His angelic host defeat Satan and his armies.

The millennial reign

This is the one-thousand-year period during which Jesus Christ and His people reign on the earth while Satan is bound in the bottomless pit. We will already be in our resurrected, glorified bodies; we will live in a world much different from the one we know:

> The wolf will live with the lamb, the leopard will lie down with the goat, the calf and the lion and the yearling together; and a little child will

lead them. The cow will feed with the bear, their young will lie down together, and the lion will eat straw like the ox. The infant will play near the cobra's den, and the young child will put its hand into the viper's nest. They will neither harm nor destroy on all my holy mountain, for the earth will be full of the knowledge of the LORD as the waters cover the sea.

—ISAIAH 11:6–9

For the first time in human history, Satan will have no influence:

And I saw an angel coming down out of heaven, having the key to the Abyss and holding in his hand a great chain. He seized the dragon, that ancient serpent, who is the devil, or Satan, and bound him for a thousand years. He threw him into the Abyss, and locked and sealed it over him, to keep him from deceiving the nations anymore until the thousand years were ended.

—REVELATION 20:1–3

The eternal heaven

This is our final step, our eternal abode. After the millennial reign and a final war, Satan will be cast forever into the lake of fire, where he will be eternally tormented (see Rev. 20:10). We will live forever with God.

The apostle John was allowed to see and hear what is to come:

And I heard a loud voice from the throne saying, "Look! God's dwelling place is now among the people, and he will dwell with them. They will be his people, and God himself will be with them and be their God. 'He will wipe every tear from their eyes. There will be no more death' or mourning or crying or pain, for the old order of things has passed away." He who was seated on the throne said, "I am making everything new!" Then he said, "Write this down, for these words are trustworthy and true."

—REVELATION 21:3–5

A wonderful future awaits God's people!

Knowing the big picture is a great encouragement to me. It reminds me that He is in charge, and I don't need to be. I can be content to see His plan unfold and enjoy the surprises only He can arrange. His timing is right and is in His hands. Eternity itself is mapped out to perfection.

This bears repeating: heaven is the beginning of life— real life in every way. I am not rushing it, but I do not want to delay it either. If I were to have another close call as I did in July 2008, my family knows which decisions I would like them to make. This is definitely not a cookie-cutter issue; what I want might not work for the next guy and his family. I only know what choices my family and I have made.

Debbie knows that if I die again, I don't want to be kept on extended life support. For her sake they can keep me alive long enough to assess my prognosis. If I could not return to a productive life, I'd just as soon go on to be with Jesus. I believe Debbie is good with that, although I doubt she will ever have to face the decision. The next time my spirit heads heavenward, I believe He will keep me for good.

⸝⸝ Chapter 10 ⸜⸜

HEAVEN'S MESSAGE of LOVE

Dear friends, let us love one another, for love comes from God. Everyone who loves has been born of God and knows God. Whoever does not love does not know God, because God is love.
1 John 4:7–8

WHEN YOU VISIT a friend's home, it is personal. A look around reveals your friend's heart. You see what he or she holds dear. Family photos, a busy kitchen, or a well-used workbench tell a story of the life that is lived behind the scenes. Things you might not have learned from sharing a cubicle at work or spending a day at the lake become plain.

I had a relationship with Jesus Christ before I died. Over the years He revealed Himself day by day. Sometimes He brought tears to my eyes or correction to my life. Even when my heart melted in His presence, He knew where I was broken. My stubbornness did not escape Him. None of my messes did either. But He loved me anyway. Every exchange helped me to see that.

But my pre-death relationship with God did not

prepare me for the impact of my trip to heaven. Once I was in His "house," I knew it, even without seeing a thing. The "atmosphere" of the place revealed His heart. It dripped with love. It oozed peace. He welcomed me home and, without a word, I was changed.

Undoing the change would be impossible. I was suited up for life in eternity. I did not know He would send me back. If I had, I would have wondered how to wear my new suit back on earth. The suit I'm talking about is love. He never asked me to turn it in because it was not something I could shed. Even with it I would remain fallible and sometimes selfish, but I was not the same human as the one who dropped dead at the rodeo.

Heaven's message is His message: love. Even on our hard-edged planet, the most universally recognizable scripture—the one we see on placards at baseball games—captures the story of God's love and what He did because of it:

> For God so loved the world that he gave his one and only Son, that whoever believes in him shall not perish but have eternal life.
> —JOHN 3:16

AMAZING LOVE

Nobody expresses love more radically than God does. No one can. And He seems never to run out of fresh ways of loving. When my daughter, Leigh, was nine years old, the Lord went above and beyond (literally) any show of love my mind could foresee.

For Leigh it was a sweet taste of just how personal God's love is. It was even sweeter because the day was special to start with—it was what would have been my dad's one hundredth birthday. The whole Vest family remembered Daddy by gathering in Celina for a big dinner and celebration. It was too big for anyone's dining room, so we held the festivities at the Celina Community Center. As families do on special occasions, we shared memories, laughed a lot, and shed a tear or two. Daddy had already been gone nearly a decade, and Leigh was now nine years old. She and Daddy hadn't had much time together, but Leigh enjoyed the celebration to the hilt.

So did my sisters. They have a way of making family events memorable. They outdid themselves for Daddy's centennial by putting together one hundred helium-filled balloons, each with a message inside for local armed services members. It was a beautiful way to honor Daddy and some hometown heroes at the same time.

At noon we went outside on the square and released all the balloons at one time. Knowing our local weather patterns, I expected them to float north, south, or east. The wind almost never blows west in our area, which is the direction of our home in Pilot Point. Yet when the balloons took off, Leigh said, "Look! The balloons are going to our house!"

She was right. The wind carried the balloons way up high and to the west! Even so, Pilot Point is thirteen miles away, so Debbie and I thought little of it. Leigh was captivated, however, and watched the sky throughout the drive home. She seemed sure, or at least determined, that she would find Grandpa's balloons at our place.

The instant we arrived home, she jumped out of the car and searched the property. Debbie and I had our doubts, but in no time flat, Leigh shouted, "Grandpa's balloon! It's here!"

Seeing how excited she was, I played along with her claim. I was not convinced we would find Grandpa's balloon, but I was sure she'd found something colorful that looked like a balloon. Surely it wasn't one of Grandpa's balloons. It couldn't be.

I dutifully humored Leigh and followed her outside. To my amazement she had found exactly what she said she found: one of Daddy's balloons! Amazingly it had made it from Celina to our house. After cruising aloft for thirteen miles, the balloon was caught on our storage tank.

I was stunned. For one thing, the logistics were all wrong. But the real kicker was where the balloon ended up. When I told Debbie, "There's a balloon on that water storage tank," we just smiled at one another, knowing that God had done something special for our little girl. But Leigh wasn't the only one God was aiming at. He pinpointed the landing place of that balloon in such a way that there could be no doubt: He had done this.

My daddy loved watermelon, so when we bought the property in Pilot Point we planted a watermelon patch just for him. His age was catching up to him by that time. He could barely get around the place, but he looked forward to those melons coming up. I'm thankful that he got to eat one before he went home to heaven. I wish he'd had time to eat more than one.

Now, on Daddy's birthday, the Lord marked the spot as only He could. Imagine the odds of a balloon from Daddy's centennial celebration landing on the water tank in his treasured watermelon patch. Who could engineer such a feat but Him? It was a sweet act of love and the perfect ending for Daddy's birthday... compliments of our Father in heaven.

DIVINE LOVE IN EARTHEN VESSELS

> But we have this treasure in earthen vessels, that the excellence of the power may be of God and not of us.
> —2 CORINTHIANS 4:7, NKJV

When the Lord pours out His love like a waterfall, it is difficult not to get wet. When I returned from heaven, I was soaked. There is no way He would send me back and not expect me to spread it around.

If there is a vessel more earthen than I am, I have not seen it yet. The people who know me best and have known me the longest know how earthen I am. The fact that I am writing a book no doubt makes some of them queasy. I am as much a "cracked pot" as any other. I didn't go to heaven in a flowing white robe; I didn't come back in one either.

Really, what does a guy like me have to share if not God's love? Even post-heaven I'm still a calf-roping cowboy who builds houses. I'm comfortable with horses, rodeos, and contracting, not pulpits. I did not come back from heaven with three-point sermons or a book of lessons to wear out the saints.

What I came back with was a deep sense of my own humanity and the fragility of life. I realize how alike we humans are and how desperately we need His love. So when He sends someone across my path, I think about how much He loves that person and remind myself that my only calling is to share that love.

Sometimes I am surprised by which people He sends my way. I ask myself, "Why would this person want to associate with me? What can I possibly offer?" The question never lingers long because I have learned that God's way of doing things is not the same as mine. It's His business. He's the One drawing the person in my direction for His reasons.

The prophet Isaiah said it better than I can:

> "For my thoughts are not your thoughts, neither are your ways my ways," declares the LORD. "As the heavens are higher than the earth, so are my ways higher than your ways and my thoughts than your thoughts."
> —ISAIAH 55:8–9

God's thinking is out of my league. And His ways—how could I have dreamed what He would do with Daddy's balloons, for example? It would never have occurred to me. Even as He was doing it, I doubted the outcome.

The same is true with the connections He sets up

between people. It is so easy to think that everyone else has his needs met. We see people who are impeccably dressed or have wads of money or talent, and we assume that we have nothing to offer them. But God sees their hearts. He knows which of their needs, hurts, or questions are still unanswered.

He also knows whom to send alongside them at just the right time. How He works all that out is way above my pay grade, as they say. All I know is, He prepares their hearts ahead of time, and it is entirely His deal. All I need to do is stay in His presence and remain willing to obey.

How else can I follow Him? When I hear His voice (He is so generous to speak to me!) and go where He sends me, what He wants to happen will happen. He gives me the words (or the smile or the friendly hello) that the person needs. He makes it easy, but that doesn't mean I always get it exactly right. Sometimes I get it almost exactly wrong. When I do, I know it—and fast. Still, He is gracious to this earthen vessel.

The best thing for me to do is to get out of His way. That doesn't mean there isn't some price to pay. There is. I cannot live with a "whatever" attitude. There is a level of accountability because it is His business. At times I feel as though I am under a microscope, not because God is nitpicky or impossible to please, but because the tenderness of another person's heart is at stake.

I have accepted the price, knowing He will lead me. And He does! He teaches me where to step in and when to stay out. There is a definite line to walk, but He gave me the desire to walk it, even though He knows how perfectly capable I am of blowing it!

He did not send me back to put on a show or act like Mr. Goody Two Shoes. I don't know what people expect of me. I don't need to know. I have nothing to prove. It's not about how loudly I sing His praises or how high I raise my hands toward heaven. This is not an acting gig. I'm the same guy I always was. I don't put on the dog about being called or being a Christian or even about going to heaven. I'm just Freddy, a cowboy who died and came back again.

Whatever He asks, I'll do it the best I know how. It is His message and His love.

Being myself seems to work out best. When people who knew me before I died find out that I'm still Freddy, they feel comfortable with me. We can still talk about life and work or whatever friends talk about. Sometimes they share the things that are on their minds. Sometimes they invite me to share what's on mine. When the Lord gives me something to say, I know they will listen, because He has prepared them ahead of time.

I never can tell whom He might send my way. Even when I am with friends at the rodeo, He works in my relationships in unexpected ways. I'm blessed to have a good friend who is also one of the premier calf ropers in the nation. He is a rising star and one in-demand cowboy. For all his celebrity, it is his humility that stands out most. Like everyone on the planet, he is a guy searching for what is real. As exciting and consuming as rodeo can be, he needs the Lord, and he knows it.

We rope together and talk a lot. Our conversations are always about the Lord first and roping second. We shoot the breeze about what God is doing and what we are going through. I have a strong sense of God's working powerfully in His life. I have told him more than once, "God's got His hand on you." I know He does, and I know it is for a reason.

For a guy in a very hot spotlight, this roper has a tender heart. He is one of the ones God brought me back to bless. He blesses me too, in a big way. Again, it is God's love and it is His business; I am honored to be a part of what He is doing. The Lord has given this young cowboy a great deal of influence in the roping world. God's love will reach many through him.

That is one of the beautiful things about God's love: it can fill up all kinds of vessels, including cowboys.

No Judgment

My father's example taught us kids a lot about how to treat others. When my brother and I brought Daddy his lunch that day and his coworkers kept cussing and speaking crudely, Daddy just moved us out of earshot. He did not reprimand the men or call them names. No doubt the men noticed what Daddy did for our sakes and got the idea soon enough.

Jesus said, "Do not judge, or you too will be judged" (Matt. 7:1). That is a heavy-duty statement, and I never want to get on the wrong side of it. I'm as prone to pointing the finger as anyone, but going to heaven helped soften me. I'm not as quick to judge as I used to be. In heaven Jesus enveloped me in total acceptance, despite my obvious shortcomings. He did not confront me with a list of my sins. He never mentioned the cussing and other things I was known for back in the day. He just loved me. I didn't need help to know I'd sinned; all I needed was His perfect love.

Recently a guy unleashed a string of cuss words during a conversation we were having. Immediately he caught himself and apologized. I said, "You don't have to apologize to me."

Making people feel uncomfortable so they'll "behave right" around me is not the reason God sent me back from heaven. I received His extreme love. How can I dole out judgment in return? When I went to heaven, it wasn't because I was a perfect man. It was because I have a perfect Savior who paid the full price for my sin. He did not withhold His love as punishment for all the times I messed up in life. Instead, He poured it out as though I had never gotten crosswise of Him.

My only assignment is to do the same and love others. Whether they are Christians or atheists is not my concern. Whether they do the right thing or treat me right is not my concern either. Even if they treat Him badly and take His name in vain, I'm not deputized as His "sin police." Writing tickets and judging people is not an option for me. God will deal with them His way because it is His business. My only responsibility is to stay focused on what He wants from me—and what He wants from me is to love them the best way I know how.

I spend a lot of time around folks who are not Christians. Most of them know about my faith. They also know I won't get on their backs. What they do in this life is between them and God. Being their friend regardless of how they act—that is my part.

Whether the guys I'm with are drinking or using bad language does not change God's love for them. It should not change mine. It is human to want to react. But with God's help, I can keep my nose from getting out of joint. I can be their friend, no matter what. When they see that they can trust me, they end up respecting me and them-selves more.

It seems counterintuitive. We like to think people need our help to do the right thing. I found the opposite to be true. When I resist judging others, they come around on their own. It may be in small ways, but it is noticeable. They might catch their language or even apologize, not because they felt pressured to do it, but because they felt comfortable enough to do it.

My usual response is, "Whatever, man. It's OK."

They know I'm not trying to change them or fix them or push religion on them. So if they find themselves feeling badly about cussing, we both know it wasn't my doing. When you get right down to it, only God can change a person anyway. If we could fix ourselves or others, Jesus's death on the cross would have been a waste of time.

The truth is, most people want to do the right thing, and most people want to be "right with God." I come across guys all the time who talk about coming to God someday. For some reason they feel the need to say it. I guess they are trying to come to grips with their sin and with the reality of eternity.

Again and again they say, "I want to clean up my life, and then I'll come to God."

I usually answer them with a couple of questions. "Why? Why don't you just accept Him and let Him show you what He wants cleaned up?"

That is what Jesus died for. One drop of His love goes a very long way.

MISSED OPPORTUNITIES TO LOVE

Years ago a young boy came into church wearing a cap. A deacon spotted him and decided to set things straight. If there had been a thought bubble over the deacon's head, it might have said: "Doesn't this whippersnapper know that gentlemen don't wear hats in church?"

The deacon took personal offense and got all over the boy's case. He was so caught up in the technicality that he forgot the main thing: to show the love of the One whose church it is. The deacon had no idea where the boy came from, what he had lived through, or what had brought him to church that day. If the boy had been raised in church, he might have known enough to remove his cap. But he wasn't raised in church, and his cap wasn't the issue. He was doing the best he knew to do. The deacon judged his best "not good enough."

For Jesus, church has nothing to do with etiquette. He said, "A new command I give you: Love one another. As I have loved you, so you must love one another. By this everyone will know that you are my disciples, if you love one another" (John 13:34–35). I doubt Jesus would have cared a lick about what was on the boy's head when his heart was at stake.

Needless to say, the boy never visited that church again. Only God knows if he ever dared enter another one. I doubt the deacon in the story had any idea how costly his reaction might be. Who knows what was on his mind that day or why the cap was so important to him? He did what we all do at some point: he judged another instead of loving. He missed the fact that a young boy in need of a Savior was trying to take a step forward. He missed the opportunity to be part of God's plan for the boy's life. He worried too much about "right" and "wrong" to do what was right himself. He missed the beautiful blessing God had teed up.

It's not only visitors who get hurt in church. People in the congregation can get burned too. Good friends of mine did. Instead of receiving love from their church family, this couple found themselves on the business end of a lawsuit. Their experience left them deeply wounded and feeling betrayed by those they had trusted. The bitter taste it left in their mouths was so bad that they decided to keep their distance from church folks altogether.

One evening they invited me to visit them when I was done roping. I knew they were hurting and struggling to understand what had happened to them. I also knew the Lord had arranged the visit, so I shared my testimony about heaven. When I finished, the husband spoke frankly. "That's all really good," he said, "and I believe every word you are saying. But nothing you said makes me want to go to church."

I understood where he was coming from. It was not my job to change his mind or make something happen. "That's fine," I said, and left it at that.

If God sent me only to plant a seed, I was satisfied to plant it. He would send someone else to water it at just the right time.

Meanwhile I pray for this couple every day, and I know the blessing works both ways: on the day I died, the husband prayed for me. One of the bright lights I saw shooting up to heaven was his prayer. I know he and his wife believe. For now their healing is still under way, and their unfortunate experience still defines for them what church is. But God will heal their wounds in His perfect timing. They will experience Jesus's love in church again someday. In the meantime I hope they will see that God's love for them never wavered and never will.

> God has said, "Never will I leave you; never will I forsake you." So we say with confidence, "The Lord is my helper; I will not be afraid. What can mere mortals do to me?"
> —HEBREWS 13:5–6

AVOIDING UNINTENDED CONSEQUENCES

Like the deacon who frightened the little boy, the church people in the second story did not set out to harm my dear friends. Often we are so afraid of being hurt or taken advantage of that we become overly defensive.

Like spooked horses, our nostrils flare and we run the risk of hurting people. The problem is that once we react, the damage is done. The only thing left to do is to allow God to set things right.

I did not share these stories to indict the church or point fingers but to invite us to think through the offenses that will surely come. We don't have to be defensive; God is our defense. (See Psalm 59:9.) If we will allow it, His love will keep us safe from danger and strife far better than we can.

Peter, the apostle who was known for speaking first and thinking later, learned about love from the Master Himself. In one of his letters Peter wrote about the enormous power inherent in love. His words, inspired by the Holy Spirit, echo Jesus's love commandment perfectly. Peter wrote: "Above all, love each other deeply, because love covers over a multitude of sins" (1 Pet. 4:8).

Jesus knew how easily we could become judgmental, even in the church. He did not take kindly to folks putting on religious airs and lording it over others. He described them harshly:

> They tie up heavy, cumbersome loads and put them on other people's shoulders, but they themselves are not willing to lift a finger to move them.... "Woe to you, teachers of the law and Pharisees, you hypocrites! You shut the door of the kingdom of heaven in people's faces. You

yourselves do not enter, nor will you let those
enter who are trying to."

—MATTHEW 23:4, 13

Jesus wasn't being mean-spirited. He wanted His
people to understand that hearts are easily broken and
eternity is in the balance. Therefore, He was much harder
on religious people who judged others than He was on
common sinners who knew nothing but sin.

When He taught at the temple one day, the religious
folks brought in a woman who was caught in adultery.
She knew what she had done and so did Jesus. But
instead of pointing out her sin, He called her accusers
on the carpet, saying, "Let any one of you who is without
sin be the first to throw a stone at her" (John 8:7).

The religious leaders knew that Jesus had their
number. They dropped their accusations and their stones
and walked away. Imagine the woman's relief and grati-
tude: she not only escaped the death sentence but also
received the pure love that would change her life.

Jesus's words must have melted her heart. They melt
mine as I read them:

> Jesus straightened up and asked her, "Woman,
> where are they? Has no one condemned you?"
> "No one, sir," she said. "Then neither do I con-
> demn you," Jesus declared. "Go now and leave
> your life of sin."
>
> —JOHN 8:10–12

After her encounter with the Savior, the woman knew what real love looked like. I can only imagine her surprise when, instead of crushing her under the weight of her sin, Jesus reached into her heart and showed her the way out.

MAKING THE MOST OF OPPORTUNITIES

> Be very careful, then, how you live—not as unwise but as wise, making the most of every opportunity, because the days are evil. Therefore do not be foolish, but understand what the Lord's will is.
> —EPHESIANS 5:15–17

Have you ever felt as if you were low on wisdom? I have. But here's God's answer: "If any of you lacks wisdom, he should ask God, who gives generously to all without finding fault, and it will be given to you" (James 1:5).

The Lord knows that His kind of love doesn't come naturally to us. He doesn't expect us to express it without His help. He will freely give us the wisdom we need to love others. He knows every heart and can show us the tender places where we need to tread gently. He will help us to recognize those who are just getting to know Him. He will reveal those who have been wounded and fear being hurt again. He will show us how our love draws others to Him and fulfills His commandment to us.

Our words and actions are more powerful than we know. Without realizing it, we greatly affect others. I realize this more every day, as I get to meet more and more people. Whether I'm at a speaking engagement or visiting with someone over a rodeo taco, I know it is an opportunity to share heaven's message of love.

It is also an opportunity to stumble. My wife, Debbie, and I pray about this often. We know Satan will try his best to trip us up, especially now that our testimony is public. I'm not worried about having my past thrown in my face. I never claimed to be a saint, and the past is dead and gone anyway. I do know this: Satan does not want one more person to be helped by my story.

So I am more determined than ever to walk circumspectly. I don't want to cooperate with Satan's schemes, not even accidentally. I trust in God, whose power is greater than all the power of the enemy. Debbie and I have put our hope in Him and Him alone. We never asked to do the things we are doing today. We were not looking for the spotlight, and I certainly was not looking to write a book! God has done it all, and we are following His lead, knowing He will keep us safe.

David's words have become ours: "He who dwells in the secret place of the Most High shall abide under the shadow of the Almighty. I will say of the LORD, 'He is my refuge and my fortress; My God, in Him I will trust'" (Ps. 91:1–2, NKJV).

My hope each day is that He would find me faithful, that I would speak His words only, that I would resist the temptation to follow my own ways, and that I would one day hear Him say these precious words: "Well done, good and faithful servant!...Come and share your master's happiness!" (Matt. 25:21).

In the meantime I do my best. While I am in this physical body, my human nature and the forces of darkness will challenge me. Jesus knows that and is always present to help me. There is no situation I cannot face with Him.

He understands everything we face in this life. He experienced all of it during His earthly walk and when the sin of the world was laid upon Him. He knows how hard it can be for us to walk in love. He knows how easily we become frustrated, even with those we love most. He knows we are desperate for His grace and mercy:

> This High Priest of ours understands our weaknesses, for he faced all of the same testings we do, yet he did not sin. So let us come boldly to the throne of our gracious God. There we will receive his mercy, and we will find grace to help us when we need it most.
> —HEBREWS 4:15–16, NLT

These words mean the world to me. I need to lay myself down at His throne daily. I need His mercy. No matter how much I love Him or how much I desire to love others, I eventually miss the mark. Bad thoughts rush into my mind; unkind words burn on the tip of my tongue. Yes, I even have moments when I think, "Man, I'd like to punch that guy's lights out."

I am still very capable of making a mess of things. I am a work in progress...and I am in His hands. I can't think of a better place to be.

⚮ Chapter 11 ⚮

MATTHEW'S LEGACY of LOVE

Precious in the sight of the LORD
is the death of his faithful servants.
PSALM 116:15

THIS IS A book about the awesome reality and hope of heaven. I cannot adequately capture it in words, yet I know the Holy Spirit will use these pages to comfort readers. That is one of the reasons for the book in the first place: to comfort the hurting, including those who mourn.

Is that you? Are you so wracked by grief, so crushed by its weight, that breathing is difficult? Has a tragic death turned your world gray and made everyday tasks seem overwhelming? You long for rest, but even sleep cannot provide it. Instead of bringing a smile to your face, beautiful memories remind you of unbearable loss. When you hear about terrible events—tornadoes, school shootings, terrorist attacks—you feel the anguish of the loved ones who were left behind. You know the pain of being awakened in the dark hours by a policeman with bad news or of taking your child to school in the morning and claiming his or her broken body from the morgue that night or of kissing your spouse good-bye, never imagining the kiss would be your last.

Whatever your story, however painful your loss, suffering doesn't have to have the last word. Your loss is real. Your sorrow is real. But heaven is real too. And so is Jesus, the healer of broken hearts:

> The Spirit of the Sovereign LORD...has sent me to bind up the brokenhearted, to proclaim freedom for the captives and release from darkness for the prisoners, to proclaim the year of the LORD's favor and the day of vengeance of our God, to comfort all who mourn.
> —ISAIAH 61:1–2

A FINE YOUNG MAN

The death of my nephew Matthew was more real than anyone in our family wanted it to be. It came without warning. There was no time to prepare. It caused great pain, the kind you may be suffering right now. This chapter is about that pain and the healing that followed. It is dedicated to you—and to Matthew.

Matthew was a typical teenage boy. He was passionate about sports and played for the McKinney Bulldogs, his high school's varsity football team in McKinney, Texas. Matthew was a linebacker and a good one, a real team player. As young as he was, he wasn't in anything for himself. He had a heart as big as Texas and always looked out for others.

Like any male his age, Matthew loved driving a pickup truck and valued the freedom it gave him. The truck got him all around town. He was an active young man, always going to games, visiting with his buddies, and stopping for pizza (which he also loved).

The pickup wasn't the only set of wheels Matthew liked, and paved roads weren't the only ones on which he drove. Matthew loved going off-road on his four-wheeler. He relished a good challenge, especially outdoors. Some of his hobbies were less risky than others. He was as happy with a fishing pole, a line, and a lake as he was driving his machines. In Matthew's book reeling in a catch was a little bit of heaven on earth.

As typical a teenager as Matthew was, he was also a very special young man. As his uncle I'm no doubt biased, but Matthew was known for some things. He was known to be caring, considerate, and well-mannered. Yes, sir; no, sir; yes, ma'am; and no ma'am were staples of his vocabulary. He loved and respected people and never met a stranger. He was known to make friends with most everyone he met. He was a joy to be around, the kind of kid who met you with a smile and left you with a bigger one. There are no perfect teens in this world, but Matthew came close.

My nephew loved his family more than he loved anything but God. At "that age" when young people want to be cool, Matthew never pulled away from his loved ones—not even the old-timers. He took pleasure in being around his family and extended family, and he made it a point to spend quality time with them. He was devoted to his mom, dad, and brother, and spent lots of time with his grandpa, whom he called Bull. Matthew and Bull always managed to get into something, whether building hunting blinds or sitting on the porch like old pals swapping stories.

That is the kind of kid Matthew was. In the few short years he had, he shared a lot of love with a lot of people. It flowed out of him naturally, as if it was the easiest thing in the world. Love is Matthew's legacy. He is still spreading it around, even though he's been in heaven for more than nine years.

A Shocking Death

Matthew's death was the kind that rocks a home, a school, and a community. It was unexpected, violent, and tragic—a story so gruesome it stays in the news. You know it is real, but you think it happens only to other people, other families, or other neighborhoods.

Matthew did not die alone. That would have been tragic enough. Knowing him, he would rather have been the only victim; but he wasn't. Matthew, two buddies, and one friend's aunt died together. In the otherwise safe city of McKinney, they were murdered execution-style.

The worst murder in the city's history happened on an ordinary night in north Texas. No one could have seen such a crime coming. For Matthew and his friends Austin and Mark, it had been a fun night among friends. Two of them were Bulldogs who had just begun to taste adulthood. The third, Mark, was only in his twenties. The three shared a meal at a local buffet-style pizza parlor, the ideal eatery for young men with hearty appetites.

After enjoying their fill of fun and food, the boys went to visit Mark's aunt, who lived nearby. The decision would prove more costly than they could have imagined. They did not know that a crime was already under way at Mark's Aunt Rosa's house. They had no suspicion of trouble when they walked in on a home invasion.

Mark's Aunt Rosa was being held hostage and interrogated by three gunmen. Rosa worked at a check-cashing store and was no doubt a familiar face in town. The gunmen wanted to schedule themselves a big payday. They demanded information from Rosa so they could rob the store.

When the boys walked in, they weren't the only ones taken by surprise. The gunmen were not expecting visitors. They were on a mission, and now their mission was in jeopardy. They hadn't planned on being outnumbered. They planned on getting what they wanted from a single indefensible victim. Perhaps they never planned on killing anyone; they certainly had not planned a multiple murder.

Nothing about that night went according to plan. Everyone had picked the wrong night to stop at Rosa's house. With three strong young men on their hands, the gunmen reacted in the worst possible way. No sooner were the friends in the door than the criminals forced them into a front bedroom. Within minutes Matthew, Austin, Mark, and Mark's Aunt Rosa had been shot.

The gunmen's robbery scheme ended in catastrophe.

Three of the victims died at the scene. Only Matthew was found alive and airlifted to Baylor University Medical Center in Dallas. He was a strong kid and clung to life just long enough to take care of one important piece of business before he died.

It was family business.

HONORING AND HONORED IN DEATH

I believe Matthew knew in his final hours that his death was near. Yet my sense is that he held on for his family's sake. Mortally wounded and incapacitated, he survived till they got to the hospital—and said good-bye to them the best he could. It meant the world to them to be with him when his earthly life ended.

The deaths of Matthew and his friends turned McKinney inside out. Locals could not imagine a crime so heinous happening in their hometown. It set everyone on edge and left a raw, gaping hole in the community. Four people had died too brutally and too soon; two of them were under the age of twenty.

As I said earlier, Matthew never met a stranger or missed an opportunity to make a friend. When he died, it seemed as if the whole city showed up to pay their respects and show their love. Young people came out in droves. Policemen, firemen, detectives, and whole families filled the large church where his memorial service was held.

Everyone was heartbroken by Matthew's passing. It

was hard for anyone to believe that they would never see him smile again. Yet in the midst of the sorrow, something bigger than physical life and death was happening. There was a reason to be joyful, and it involved eternity. I don't know how many people answered the altar call at Matthew's memorial service, but a good number came to faith in Christ that day. Even if it had been only one, I know Matthew would have been thrilled.

The support for Matthew and his friends did not end with their funerals. Every year local friends perform some type of tribute, often at Matthew's parking place at the high school. One ongoing tradition since Matthew's death involves his jersey number, 34. Whenever his friends see his number anywhere, they photograph it and post it on Facebook. To them it is a sign of their beloved friend. Whether the number appears on a digital thermometer, a street sign, or a mailbox, someone will capture the shot and share it online. Matthew's friends have been surprised to see how often the number 34 comes up.

Matthew has also been honored on a family website. His parents and brother miss him terribly. His mother admits she was devastated by the loss of her son, but she can also testify that God's love has been poured out, and her faith has grown stronger in the years since his passing. Matthew's mom understands what Paul wrote about under the inspiration of the Holy Spirit:

> We also glory in our sufferings, because we know that suffering produces perseverance;

> perseverance, character; and character, hope. And
> hope does not put us to shame, because God's
> love has been poured out into our hearts through
> the Holy Spirit, who has been given to us.
>
> —ROMANS 5:3–5

REACHING TO AFGHANISTAN

In the months and years since their loss Matthew's family has received many notes, cards, and letters of condolence and testimony. His mom shared with me one of the more unusual and touching letters that came in. It was from a friend of Matthew's who served in Afghanistan.

The young soldier described a fierce battle in which his platoon came under fire and he was separated from his comrades. In the thick of the fight he was unsure of which way to go and what to do. He was desperate for insight; without it he would not live to rejoin his platoon and fight another day.

The young man claimed that Matthew appeared to him at that moment. Before you get upset, please know that I don't believe God's people become angels in heaven. I'm not promoting any nonbiblical phenomenon or New Age experience. I'm just reporting what this young warrior saw.

I do not know what happened on the battlefield that day, but I do know this: God meets people where they are by whatever method He chooses. I also know that God has sent angels to take on the form of human beings and communicate with them. Two such angels went to Lot's aid in Sodom, as described in Genesis chapter 19. They are the same two angels that accompanied the Lord as He visited Abraham. (See Genesis 18.)

Whatever the explanation for the soldier's experience in Afghanistan, it certainly got his attention and blessed Matthew's grieving family.

A Mother's Peace

Matthew's mother grieves for him to this day, as any mother would. Parents expect their children to bury them, not the other way around. Any parent who has lost a child will tell you that it is the most difficult life experience of all.

Matthew's mom and dad endured every parent's worst nightmare. They faced it the only way you can: one day at a time. At some point Matthew's mom saw my video testimony about heaven[1] and took great comfort in it. What she had always known became more real—her son was a Christian basking in the presence of his Lord and Savior, Jesus Christ. She never wonders where he is. She knows he is in heaven. She also knows that if Matthew were given the chance to return to this life, he would turn it down.

Matthew loved his family. His mom knows that well. She also knows that nothing on this earth can compare with heaven. She would give almost anything to see him again, but she can't—at least not in this life. For now she is satisfied knowing she will see her son again someday. Scripture promises her she will:

Brothers and sisters, we do not want you to be uninformed about those who sleep in death, so that you do not grieve like the rest of mankind, who have no hope. For we believe that Jesus died and rose again, and so we believe that God will bring with Jesus those who have fallen asleep in him.

—1 THESSALONIANS 4:13–14

MATTHEW AND
THE TIMELINE

In chapter 9 I described the timeline the Lord shared with me, along with several scriptures about God's knowing us in eternity. Ephesians 1:4 says that "he chose us in him before the creation of the world to be holy and blameless in his sight." In Jeremiah 1:5 God explains His calling to the prophet: "Before I formed you in the womb I knew you, before you were born I set you apart."

Below is the passage we read from the Book of Romans, with an additional verse for good measure. It describes the believer's beautiful journey:

And we know that in all things God works for the good of those who love him, who have been called according to his purpose. For those God foreknew he also predestined to be conformed to the image of his Son, that he might be the firstborn among many brothers and sisters. And those he predestined, he also called; those he

called, he also justified; those he justified, he
also glorified.
—ROMANS 8:28–30

Not only were we called, justified, and destined to be
glorified, but we were also called according to His purpose. God has wrapped us so tightly in His care that He
works all things for our good!

How is that possible? Could God bring anything good
from a quadruple murder? What benefit could possibly
come from such a horrific event? The human answer is,
"None! The death of Matthew and three others is evil. It
is horrendous. No good can come of it."

I understand the sentiment. Certainly the act that
caused four deaths was evil. Someone looking to make
fast money slaughtered my nephew and three others. It
is sin...wrong...period.

Yet Matthew's death precipitated salvation for the
living. Some people came to Christ as a direct result of
the murders. Their lives were transformed. Instead of
heading toward eternity in hell, they changed direction.
Now they are promised eternity with Jesus. That is a
very good outcome that came at a very great cost. I'm
not saying that three gunmen killed Matthew so people
would be saved from hell. I am saying that God brought
good out of an unbearable tragedy.

There is another thing, and it involves the timeline:
God was not caught by surprise when four innocents
were murdered in McKinney. He is omniscient; He saw
it coming. The scriptures we just revisited show that God

205

sees it all—past, present, and future—before it plays out in what we call time. Nothing catches Him off guard—nothing. Notice what He said: "I am God, and there is none like me. I make known the end from the beginning, from ancient times, what is still to come. I say, 'My purpose will stand, and I will do all that I please'" (Isa. 46:9–10).

I believe God had a purpose for Matthew's life that was not thwarted by death. The way I see it, God had a purpose in Matthew's ending. Not everyone will agree with my view, and that's OK with me. I'm not trying to force my views on anyone but only share what I feel God wants me to share. My perspective is part of that calling.

Matthew's story, including his life and death, has made it possible for many people to be touched by the Lord. There is no way to know how many people at this point, but I believe the numbers are beyond counting. To think that his death was as significant as his life is a bitter pill for those of us who loved him. In terms of eternity his death may prove to be even more impactful than his life. His story now reaches many more people than he ever knew during his lifetime.

Even though his life was much shorter than any of us wanted it to be, I believe God's purpose for him was fulfilled.

Not My Will but Yours

Have you read the prayer Jesus prayed in the Garden of Gethsemane the night before He was crucified? Three

Gospels give similar accounts of it. Below is a selection from Luke. Notice Jesus's warning to His disciples and His sincere words to the Father:

> Jesus went out as usual to the Mount of Olives, and his disciples followed him. On reaching the place, he said to them, "Pray that you will not fall into temptation." He withdrew about a stone's throw beyond them, knelt down and prayed, "Father, if you are willing, take this cup from me; yet not my will, but yours be done." An angel from heaven appeared to him and strengthened him. And being in anguish, he prayed more earnestly, and his sweat was like drops of blood falling to the ground.
>
> —LUKE 22:39–44

In Matthew's and Mark's accounts Jesus warned the disciples about our vulnerability to temptation. He said, "The spirit is willing, but the flesh is weak" (Matt. 26:41; Mark 14:38). If I might paraphrase Jesus's words, I believe He was saying, "Neither My body nor My mind want to go through what I am destined for, but My spirit is strong and willing to complete My assignment."

Jesus the human being did not want to die on the cross. Neither His mind nor His body welcomed the horror of crucifixion. So twice He asked the Father to change His mind about it. What human being would choose such a death? None would choose it based on the flesh, but Jesus's spirit was willing to accept what God had for Him to do, despite the suffering involved.

It was not an easy thing. Jesus suffered greatly, and He saw the pain coming. Luke described Jesus's agony at Gethsemane as He contemplated what lay ahead: "An angel from heaven appeared to him and strengthened him. And being in anguish, he prayed more earnestly, and his sweat was like drops of blood falling to the ground" (Luke 22:43–44). Imagine being under such pressure that you would sweat blood!

Jesus saw tribulation ahead, but He also saw the reward of His obedience. The writer of Hebrews shows us this brighter side of Jesus's sacrifice. It explains what Jesus knew in His spirit about His impending death. It helps us to see what He saw:

> Let us run with perseverance the race marked out for us, fixing our eyes on Jesus, the pioneer and perfecter of faith. For the joy set before him he endured the cross, scorning its shame, and sat down at the right hand of the throne of God.
> —HEBREWS 12:1–2

Just as Jesus faced His moment of reckoning in the garden, I believe my nephew Matthew faced a similar moment. As much as he loved his mom and dad, his brother, his grandparents, and others, the real Matthew, the spirit within him, willingly accepted what God had for him to do.

Matthew would not have wanted to leave so soon. He was enjoying life. He loved people. He had a bright future, and he was excited about it. He looked forward to being married and starting a family. He would have been a terrific husband and a loving father. He wanted to live to an old age. Yet I believe he followed Jesus's example: he committed his spirit into God's hands. He was not expecting to be faced with such a decision so soon, but Matthew's spirit said, "I am willing." In a split second of time, I believe my nephew saw the timeline of eternity. I believe he saw the joy set before him and opted in.

Today an unknown number of people have become new creations (see 2 Corinthians 5:17) because they heard about Jesus at Matthew's funeral and beyond. Knowing how Matthew loved Jesus and loved people, I doubt anything could make him happier.

Even so, Matthew's death caused tremendous sorrow and soul-searching for those he left behind. They will never forget Matthew or his death, but they know that the real Matthew is alive and well. He is in paradise being comforted by Jesus Himself! That is cause for rejoicing!

GOD'S GREATER PURPOSE

God's Word is clear: We are not to harm others but to love them. (See Exodus 20:13; Romans 13:9–10.) That is the greatest commandment of all. Yet we live in a depraved world in which many people's hearts are hardened. Jesus told His disciples ahead of time: "Because of the increase of wickedness, the love of most will grow cold" (Matt. 24:12).

It is happening before our eyes. Ten minutes of the evening news is enough to tell us that. When God created

Adam and Eve, He never intended for them and those who came after them to fall into sin. But they did. In His redeeming love He desires to bring good from every circumstance, however negative or hard to take.

I believe that Matthew—not the body but the spirit— was in such close relationship with the Holy Spirit that he said, "Lord, I'll do whatever You have for me to do." In the eternal picture seen in Romans 8:30 and elsewhere I can glimpse what I believe Matthew saw—God's plan from before the foundations of the world. Despite the earthly desires Matthew held dear, his spirit was willing to move on, and Matthew received his reward.

Everyone who knew and loved Matthew, especially his immediate family and closest friends, misses him terribly. They will never forget the night they received the terrible news. Yet they are at peace knowing that Matthew is in eternity, where they will see him one day.

You may be experiencing a terrible loss and the great pain that goes with it. I cannot promise that your suffering will end today or that you will ever stop missing your loved one. Yet I pray with all my heart that Matthew's story has given you hope and the comfort Jesus died to give you.

> He was despised and rejected by mankind, a man of suffering, and familiar with pain. Like one from whom people hide their faces he was despised, and we held him in low esteem. Surely he took up our pain and bore our suffering.
>
> —ISAIAH 53:3–4

~Chapter 12~

NOTHING IS MORE REAL

But as it is written: "Eye has not seen, nor ear heard, nor have entered into the heart of man the things which God has prepared for those who love Him." But God has revealed them to us through His Spirit. For the Spirit searches all things, yes, the deep things of God.
1 CORINTHIANS 2:9–10, NKJV

H EAVEN IS REAL, even more real than rodeo. I have shared a little about the latter and a book's worth about the former. Heaven is truly an unmatched place, but it is about much more than eternal bliss; it is about destiny.

The word *destiny* has many shades of meaning. What I'm talking about is not the "clawing your way up the ladder of success" kind of destiny, or the stockpiling of cash for a Fiji retirement. It's not about being the world's best calf roper. It's not even about winning the Nobel Peace Prize. The destiny I'm talking about is the "big rodeo"—eternal destiny. Compared to it, everything else looks small.

Do you remember Solomon's words? He said, "[God]

has also set eternity in the human heart" (Eccles. 3:11). That is a mouthful, because eternity gives real meaning to life and death. Worries and fears shrink down to size when you see them through God's lens. Even death cannot force you to fear when your spirit sees what "no eye has seen" (1 Cor. 2:9).

God reveals the things He prepared ahead of time "for those who love Him." He doesn't reveal them to our senses but to the "real us"—the spirit He breathed into us:

> But God has revealed them to us through His Spirit. For the Spirit searches all things, yes, the deep things of God. For what man knows the things of a man except the spirit of the man which is in him? Even so no one knows the things of God except the Spirit of God. Now we have received, not the spirit of the world, but the Spirit who is from God, that we might know the things that have been freely given to us by God.
> —1 CORINTHIANS 2:10–12, NKJV

When the Holy Spirit communicates with your spirit, you "see" what He has freely given you! It is much more than I am called to share or even could share. Now, just a few things remain. They are the things I would say if we were talking over coffee or a couple of rodeo hot dogs. Like everything I've already said, I pray that these things will strengthen and comfort you.

The Fear of Death

Millions of people fear death. The bottom line is that death is what most people fear most. It's not surprising. We instinctively value life and don't surrender it easily. We also like to be in control, so death naturally goes against our grain. And we sure don't like venturing into "the unknown," especially when there are no do-overs.

Fearing death does not make you a wimp. Even strong and seemingly fearless people fear death. Frankly, if you are not a Christian, you have every reason to fear death. You will live forever, but it won't be in heaven. The world talks about heaven as if everyone will be reunited there one day. I wish that were true, but it's not—not unless you receive Jesus as your Savior and accept His sacrifice for your sins.

Friend, the question is not whether you will live forever. The question is where. Because of Christ's finished work, you get to choose. You don't have to fear death one more day. Jesus offered freedom from this slavery two thousand years ago:

> Since the children have flesh and blood, [Jesus] too shared in their humanity so that by his death he might break the power of him who holds the power of death—that is, the devil—and free those who all their lives were held in slavery by their fear of death.
> —Hebrews 2:14–15

Jesus broke the power of death. All you have to do is say, "Yes, Jesus, be my Lord and Savior," and heaven will be your home.[1]

It's the best decision you will ever make, but don't expect everyone to slap you a high five for making it. A cowboy friend of mine often mentions God on Twitter. He has many, many fans, but not everyone wants to hear about God. Sometimes folks get ugly about his tweets. They are not satisfied until they trash God, my friend, and the horse he rides!

He asked me for advice about how to handle these situations. Every Christian runs into them at some point, but they are even more complicated when they are public. Some people believe that talk of God and heaven is for idiots. Some are atheists who are "religiously" against the idea of God's existence. I'm not a psychologist, but I would guess that the fear of death is involved. It's not easy to hear about eternity when, deep down, you know that hell is real too.

All I could tell my friend was how I handle similar situations. It takes more than one hundred forty characters to talk it through, but I begin by asking the person, "What happens when you die?"

Atheists usually say, "Nothing. When I die, it's over."

"OK," I answer. "You say there's no God. I disagree with you, but if you're right, it doesn't matter what I believe. Whatever happens to you at death will happen to me too: nothing. Our carcasses will rot in the grave, and the world will be done with us."

The atheist likes my agreement until I continue: "Now

let's look at this from my perspective. I believe God is real, and I will spend eternity with Him. If I'm right, we'll both live forever, but you'll spend eternity in hell. If you're a betting man, those are the worst odds you'll ever play."

You don't have to play those odds. Jesus died so you wouldn't have to. Accept His offer, and the fear of death will be finished. Your eternal destiny will play out in heaven, the place Jesus invited you to call home.

THE FEAR OF DYING

Over the years I've realized that the fear of death is often lumped together with the fear of dying. This explains why even some Christians are uneasy about the end of life. It is not death that they fear. They know where death leads, and they know it is good. But the act of dying is another story.

The concern is perfectly natural. For one thing, most of us don't get to take a test run. We live our entire lives not knowing what to expect in our final moments. Most of us don't like surprises much, and some of us have another hurdle to overcome: we know someone whose death was slow and painful. We file the terrible memory in our "I hope that doesn't happen to me" file, knowing full well that it might.

Do you fear the act of dying? If you are a Christian, you can take hope in the bigger picture—eternity with Him. You might know someone who suffered greatly. You might also know someone like my daddy, whose death was glorious. The truth is, you don't know what your dying moments will be like. But you can know beyond the shadow of a doubt that your death will be the beginning of the most awesome life of all.

Paul wrote that death has no sting (1 Cor. 15:55). He was right. He quoted the prophet Hosea, who prophesied about the powerlessness of the grave for the believer: "I will deliver this people from the power of the grave; I will redeem them from death. Where, O death, are your plagues? Where, O grave, is your destruction?" (Hosea 13:14).

When you accept the redemption purchased by Jesus Christ, the grave cannot hold you in fear now or hold you in darkness later. Not only that, but God will also carry you through the act of dying with peace and divine comfort.

> "My grace is sufficient for you, for my power is made perfect in weakness." Therefore I will boast all the more gladly about my weaknesses, so that Christ's power may rest on me.
> —2 CORINTHIANS 12:9

THE FEAR OF LOVED ONES DYING

Losing a loved one is as tough as nails. Without hesitating, I admit that the mere thought of it tempts me to fear. I don't think I've lived a single day without the thought coming to mind. Like any parent and husband, I want the best for my family. My desire is for them to live the lives they dream of living to the fullest and to the very end. I don't want their lives cut short, and I don't want to live without them either.

That is human nature and human love. We don't ever want to be separated from loved ones; we don't even want to imagine what it would be like. We know that our time together in this world can't last forever, but we cherish it, and hope that, somehow, it might.

Have you lost someone to a terminal illness? Is someone in your family terminally ill now? If so, you know how difficult it is. The diagnosis is shocking enough. The roller coaster of emotions that follows is exhausting. It helps somewhat to have time to prepare for the end, and it helps if you know your loved one is heaven bound. But the good-byes are never painless. If we are honest, we sometimes pray the person will linger, even when all they really want is to graduate to heaven.

My cousin Jack and his family lived through this scenario when his twenty-six-year-old daughter was diagnosed with terminal cancer. Hollie was married and had two small children at the time. Instead of enjoying precious moments around the dinner table with her husband and children, she was hospitalized and suffering tremendous pain. It was as tough a battle as this life can offer.

As God would have it, a relative gave Jack my video testimony of heaven.[2] His heart was breaking at the time, but seeing the video gave him great peace. It affected him so much that he decided to show it to Hollie. She was

217

already a Christian, but the video ministered powerfully to her. She knew in her spirit that heaven was her home, and the thought of leaving got easier. She did not want to leave her husband and children. No young mother wants to do that. Yet my testimony eased her mind and gave her fresh hope. I'm thankful God sent me back from heaven, if only to help Hollie.

The day after Jack showed his daughter the video, I sensed the Lord calling me to visit her. When I arrived at the hospital, Jack spotted me in the hallway. We hugged and talked a little bit before entering his daughter's room.

"It's not right for a parent to bury a child, Freddy," he said.

"No, Jack. There is nothing easy about it. It's not easy at all." There isn't much you can say to a father whose child is near death.

"She had peace with the video," Jack said. "She's really hurting...in a lot of pain. The doctors said she has another two or three months..." his voice trailed off.

Jack was torn. No doubt he hoped to have his daughter around for as long as possible. Yet he knew she was suffering greatly.

I understood his turmoil. "Jack," I said, "when God is ready for her to come home, and she's ready to go, and you and the rest of the family are ready to release her, she will go home."

"I don't want her to suffer," Jack said.

With that we went into his daughter's room. She had been drifting in and out of consciousness, but when we walked in she said, "Hello," smiled, and that was it. She was too heavily medicated to visit with us anymore.

Before I left, I talked to Jack about the need for families to release their loved ones. Even those who are in extreme pain will hang on for the sake of the family. They want to go home but don't feel free to do so. Their families don't always realize the need to verbalize their agreement with the person's decision to leave. Dying people need to know that they are not disappointing the ones they love most. The last thing they want is to cause more pain.

I can't know for sure what was in Hollie's heart, but I do know that she went home the very next day. The end of her mortal life happened God's way and in His timing. She and her family were ready, and heaven was ready too.

During the family's visitation night before the funeral, Jack praised the Lord for the sweet way in which his daughter had passed on. He asked me, "Doesn't she look peaceful, Freddy?"

"She sure does," I replied. And she did. Hollie's suffering was over forever.

Her family misses her terribly, but the sting of her death was swallowed in the promise of eternity. Hollie got a head start on real living, and she will welcome her loved ones to heaven someday.

FEELING FORGOTTEN BY GOD

When I drifted from God years ago, some folks wrote me off and thought God had done the same. But that is man's way, not His way.

When the nation of Israel turned its back on God and worshipped idols, they suffered many consequences. They endured brutal captivity and became a scattered people, separated from the land of God's promise. They knew they had sinned against God repeatedly, and they thought He had written them off for it.

But Israel was suffering the effects of their own choices. God had not turned His back on them. In fact, He could not, and He told them so!

> But Zion said, "The LORD has forsaken me, the Lord has forgotten me."
>
> "Can a mother forget the baby at her breast and have no compassion on the child she has borne? Though she may forget, I will not forget you! See, I have engraved you on the palms of my hands."
>
> —ISAIAH 49:14–16

God never forgets us or pulls away from us. The only distance we ever sense is the one we create in our minds. He never moves, but we do. His Word is His bond: "Those he predestined, he also called; those he called, he also justified; those he justified, he also glorified" (Rom. 8:30). His love stands, even when ours wavers.

Do you feel forgotten by Him? Do you think He has changed His mind about you?

He hasn't! If you are His, He has you engraved on the palms of His hands. And if you aren't, you can be. If you feel abandoned, bring your feelings to Him. His throne of grace is always open! Just ask Him where you strayed. Then surrender to Him once again. You can say: "God, I'm ready to obey whatever You tell me to do. Until I hear from You, I'll stay right here, reading Your Word and worshipping You. I will listen until I know how to proceed. Then I will listen and worship You some more."

I'm not a Bible scholar or a faith giant, but I know this much about God: He is love. He created us in love and He will keep us in love. If we seek Him, He will reveal His plans for us. By His grace we can offer ourselves in spiritual worship as living sacrifices pleasing to Him (Rom. 12:1–2). Then, when our earthly time is done, He will take us home to be with Him forever.

I can almost hear someone saying, "It's no use. God can't use me anymore."

Are those your words? Is that what you think? Do you believe that you are washed up with God or too far gone to be used by Him?

It's a lie! Anytime that thought starts rolling around in your head, you can be certain it is Satan talking. God is not hung up on your past. He cares about you, not your past. What happened is no surprise or secret to Him. He knows everything you ever did, and He knows what caused you to do it. Even before the foundation of the world, He knew how your life would play out. And still He sent Jesus to the cross—for you.

If you have a heart for Him and will trust Him to love you just as you are, He will use your past for His glory. I am the poster boy of this truth. No one was more "out there" than I was, and He is using me. It never ceases to amaze me. It reminds me of just how deep and wide His love is.

God isn't holding a checklist against you. He is waiting to use you for His glory. All He wants is a willing heart. If you offer Him that, He will give you your assignment for this life. You won't need to be perfect, and you won't have to make it happen. Just offer what you have, and be ready when He calls. He will call!

THANKFUL FOR THE JOURNEY

Until I return to heaven for good, I will not fully understand the amazing journey God has allowed me to take. Yet I know that even if I live another fifty years, heaven will be in my heart.

Nothing is more real.

Every time I stop to think that He awaits me in heaven, my heart fills up with His love again. As if that were not enough, He has given me the awesome privilege of reaching out to you and others whom I hope to meet in heaven someday. I cannot know what sharing my story with you has accomplished, but I know it was His doing. That is all I need to know.

Remember—your life will not end with your last

breath. When your spirit leaves your body, your real life will begin. I pray you will choose God and the real heaven He prepared for you. And I pray that King David's words would be yours:

> Day and night I'll stick with GOD; I've got a good thing going and I'm not letting go. I'm happy from the inside out, and from the outside in, I'm firmly formed. You canceled my ticket to hell— that's not my destination! Now you've got my feet on the life path, all radiant from the shining of your face. Ever since you took my hand, I'm on the right way.
>
> —PSALM 16:8–11, THE MESSAGE

NOTES

CHAPTER 1
COWBOYS AND ANGELS

1. Some details of the author's account are also noted in Amy Reid, "A Rodeo Cowboy's Fight to Survive," CBN.com, http://www.cbn.com/700club/features/amazing/AR99_Freddy_Vest.aspx (accessed May 27, 2013).

2. *Flanking* is "a term used to describe the procedure of grabbing the calf's leg with one hand and its underbelly with the other and then flipping the calf." Kimberly King, *Calf Roping* (New York: The Rosen Publishing Group, 2006), 40.

3. A calf "takes a tie" when the roper binds three of the calf's legs.

CHAPTER 2
REARED IN THE FAITH

1. Junior was not a title or suffix to my brother's name. His first name was Morris Junior.

CHAPTER 5
A SHORT RIDE TO HEAVEN

1. A simple prayer is all you need to start a new life with Jesus as your Savior and Lord. You can use your own words, or you can pray the following: *Jesus, I repent of my sins and I receive You as my Savior and Lord. I believe that You died for my sake, to cleanse me of all sin. Thank You for Your precious sacrifice and for making me a new creation. Amen.*

The following scriptures explain more about this prayer: "If you confess with your mouth the Lord Jesus and believe in your heart that God has raised Him from the dead, you will be saved. For with the heart one believes unto righteousness, and with the mouth confession is made unto salvation" (Rom. 10:9–10, NKJV); "If anyone is in Christ, he is a new creation; old things have passed away; behold, all things have become new" (2 Cor. 5:17, NKJV).

CHAPTER 6
BACK IN THE SADDLE

1. Reid, "A Rodeo Cowboy's Fight to Survive."

CHAPTER 7
THE WHY AND THE WHERE

1. "Richard Bach Quotes," Brainy Quote, http://www
.brainyquote.com/quotes/authors/r/richard_bach.html (accessed
May 23, 2013).
2. Reid, "A Rodeo Cowboy's Fight to Survive."

CHAPTER 8
THREE HEAVENS

1. Robert Jamieson, A. R. Fausset, and David Brown, "Commentary on Revelation 21," Blue Letter Bible, http://tinyurl
.com/kum4574 (accesed March 31, 2014).

CHAPTER 9
ETERNITY IN US

1. Reid, "A Rodeo Cowboy's Fight to Survive."

CHAPTER 11
MATTHEW'S LEGACY OF LOVE

1. Reid, "A Rodeo Cowboy's Fight to Survive."

CHAPTER 12
NOTHING IS MORE REAL

1. A simple prayer is all you need to start a new life with
Jesus as your Savior and Lord. You can use your own words, or
you can pray the following: *Jesus, I repent of my sins and I receive
You as my Savior and Lord. I believe that You died for my sake, to
cleanse me of all sin. Thank You for Your precious sacrifice and for
making me a new creation. Amen.*
2. Reid, "A Rodeo Cowboy's Fight to Survive."

EMPOWERED
TO RADICALLY CHANGE
YOUR WORLD

11843